The Books of Elizabeth Bowen

NOVELS
A World of Love (*1955*)
The Last September (*1929, 1952*)
The Heat of the Day (*1949*)
The Death of the Heart (*1939*)
The House in Paris (*1936*)
To the North (*1933*)

SHORT STORIES
Ivy Gripped the Steps (*1946*)
Look at All Those Roses (*1941*)

NON-FICTION
Seven Winters AND *Afterthoughts* (*1962*)
A Time in Rome (*1960*)
The Shelbourne Hotel (*1951*)
Collected Impressions (*1950*)
Bowen's Court (*1942*)

These are BORZOI BOOKS, *published in
New York by* ALFRED A. KNOPF

SEVEN WINTERS

&

AFTERTHOUGHTS

SEVEN WINTERS
Memories of a Dublin Childhood

AFTERTHOUGHTS
Pieces on Writing

BY

ELIZABETH BOWEN

New York: Alfred·A·Knopf

1 9 6 2

L. C. catalog card number: 62–11050

THIS IS A BORZOI BOOK,
PUBLISHED BY ALFRED A. KNOPF, INC.

FIRST EDITION

Seven Winters was first published in a limited edition in Dublin in 1942 by The Cuala Press, and in London in 1943 by Longmans, Green & Co., Ltd.

"Exclusion" and the section entitled "Broadcasts" are published here for the first time.

T O

DEREK HILL

FOREWORD

SEVEN WINTERS *could be called a fragment of auto-biography. At the same time, I look on it as a self-contained work, for it is as much of my life story as I intend to write—that is, to write directly. Through most fiction is to be traced the thread of the author's own experiences, no doubt. But the early years of child-hood contain most others: as we now know they are in part the cause of, in part the key to, what is to follow. No years, subsequently, are so acute. The happenings in Seven Winters are those that I shall remain certain of till I die. Here is the external world as I first saw it. As a marvel it was at the time sufficient. Something of the marvel, however, something of the amazement, recurs*

*when I write or read. For this reason, there is for me
a link between* Seven Winters *and the rest of this book,
which I have entitled* Afterthoughts.

*Easy to be wise after the event. For the writer writ-
ing is eventful; one might say, it is in itself eventfulness.
More than any activity, it involves thought, but the
thought involved in it is by nature captive, specialized,
and intense. One may not know what one has (finally)
written till one has finished it—and then, only after a
term of time. Then begins a view of the whole, a more
perceptive or comprehensive vision; but too late. However, fortunately for authors they are seldom prey to
regret. They seldom look back, for they are usually engaged upon something else.*

*Reading is eventful also. It too engages the faculties,
so closely that reflection is only possible when the book
has been finished and put down. At a first reading, one
has little but reflexes—or so I find.*

*The only criticism of which I am capable is a form
of afterthought; whether this is applied to work of my
own or the work of others. The undertaking to write a
review or preface invites reflectiveness—of which the
results, the decisions or discoveries, may not always be
easy to give form to. This book contains pieces upon
which I might not have embarked had I not been asked
to; though I must add that for me the actual writing
had an inherent pleasure. Also, discussion of my different stories, recalling the circumstances and time at their*

start surrounding them, has come to be autobiography in an indirect form.

My so-called "Reflections," in this book's second section, risk being less reflective than didactic, possibly theoretic. Some arose out of my work with students of writing, and are my ideas of the craft, or notes on the process. Some are answers to questions, or statements made because, at some place or time or another, it was required that they should be.

The broadcasts I have left as they were spoken. Bear in mind that, being for the air, they address themselves to the hearer rather than the reader. To try to smooth out their language would, I considered, be a mistake.

Old Headington, Oxford
1962

CONTENTS

xi

CONTENTS

Seven Winters

MEMORIES OF A DUBLIN CHILDHOOD

HERBERT PLACE

THE FIRST three weeks of my life were weeks of June
—the only June I spent in Dublin until the summer
when I was twenty-one. I was born in the room, designed for a back drawing-room, that was my mother's
bedroom at 15 Herbert Place. Its one high window
looked out—as I remember later—across mews at the
backs of the houses in Herbert Street. That is the kind
of outlook that no season affects. But the nursery that
waited for me a floor higher was in the front of the
house: under its windows lay the road, the canal, and
a row of trees. So I must once have seen those Herbert
Place trees in full leaf, though with the eyes of a baby
only just born.

After that June, the existence of their first child set

3

up for my father and mother a new routine: every spring she took me down to the country, and we remained out of Dublin till late October, only returning in time to see the leaves fall and lie clotted on the sleepy and dark canal.

Number 15 Herbert Place, in fact, was a winter house; early dusks, humid reflections, and pale sunshine seemed a part of its being. I used to believe that winter lived always in Dublin, while summer always lived in County Cork. By taking the train from Kingsbridge station to Mallow one passed from one season's kingdom into the other's: hawthorn was always in flower along the hedges as we drove from Mallow to our own gates. When they first made me understand that I had been born in Dublin, I said: "But how?—my birthdays are always at Bowen's Court." A house where a child no longer is is virtually rolled up and put away. So by having been born where I had been born in a month in which that house did not exist, I felt that I had intruded on some no-place.

It is true that the lateness of my arrival had thrown out a number of summer plans. I was born nearly four weeks beyond the expected date, and the delay kept my relations rooted to Dublin when they might have otherwise gone away. One of my mother's sisters had hurried back from the Continent very much too soon, as it turned out, and for weeks the friends of the family had been greeting each other with "Any news of Robert?" My father was the head of his family; male heirs had not yet failed for the County Cork

4

property; he and my mother had been married for nine years, and now that a child was coming they expected a son. The rule of names with the Bowens was a simple one: since the first Colonel Henry Bowen, a Welshman, had come to Ireland with the Cromwellian army and been granted the lands of Farahy, County Cork, there had been a long run of Henrys, with an occasional John, till an heiress bride, Jane Cole, in the eighteenth century, brought in the name of Robert from her own people. John (at least as the heir's name) was then dropped out, and since the building of Bowen's Court with Jane Cole's money the first male Bowen in each generation had been christened either Robert or Henry. My grandfather had been Robert, my father Henry—there was no doubt which name was waiting for me. Be it said that my father and mother, when I was at last with them, did not once murmur at my being a girl. They agreed to call me Elizabeth, the most constant Bowen feminine name. For some time they expected Robert to follow, but no Robert ever did follow: I was an only child.

My father's setting up of a house in Dublin had been a departure from the Bowen tradition. His ancestors came as youths to Trinity College, and afterwards made business or pleasure trips to the capital, but County Cork had always been our locale. My father had been expected to live at Bowen's Court and give himself up to being a landowner. But towards the end of his time at college he had found that he wished to have a profession; he read law and was called to the Bar in 1887, three years before his marriage. My grandfather had felt bitter about this: he felt that the proper management of one's estate was in itself a full and worthy profession, and that my father, by taking up work in Dublin, was only showing himself a new kind of absentee. Bowen's Court, in his view, was likely to suffer from Henry's divided life. Robert Bowen, in whom this foreboding never abated, died the year after his heir was called to the Bar, so the shadow and pain of the disagreement must have overcast the opening of my father's career. On his choice itself my father never looked back: he had found the right outlet for his intellectual powers; he delighted in law; he enjoyed the sociability of the Law Library, and he had loved Dublin since his Trinity College days. Indeed, no chance of birth or sense of heir's obligations could ever have turned my father into a countryman.

For the first years after their marriage he and my mother lived in lodgings in Upper Pembroke Street, going for his vacations to Bowen's Court. After that, they decided to set up a Dublin home. Something drew them to Herbert Place—that row of smallish, light-brown brick Georgian houses with high steps, fronting on the canal. It lies below Baggot Street Bridge, on the city side of the water: a sawmill used to be on the other side.

For this new home they had to buy carpets, curtains, a chesterfield sofa, beds. The rest of the furniture that they needed was brought up to Dublin from

Bowen's Court. That house had been lavishly furnished for a large family, and much that was in it, my
mother saw, could be spared. So, shapely Sheraton
chairs, tables, cupboards, mirrors, and sideboards that
had been the work of Cork cabinet-makers in the
eighteenth century now occupied Dublin rooms of,
roughly, their own date. They were eked out with
"pieces"—most notably a carved cherrywood writing-
table—that had been given my mother as wedding
presents, also by some antiques of unknown birthplace that she had bought at low prices along the
Dublin quays. The family silver, also, was divided
between the winter and summer homes. Herbert
Place, for my father, was more than a winter house:
he stayed on there by himself till he came to join us at
the close of the Trinity term.

My mother was not a County Cork woman, nor,
like most of the earlier Bowen brides, did she come
from the counties of Tipperary or Limerick. Her
family, the Colleys, were originally of Castle Carbery,
County Kildare; they had been in Ireland since Queen
Elizabeth's reign. The Castle itself was now since
some time in ruins, and most of the land round it had
been sold. The Colleys lived at the time of my mother's marriage (and continued to live until I was four
years old) at Mount Temple, Clontarf—a Victorian
house that, from the top of its lawns, looked with its
many windows out across Dublin Bay. My father, as a
young Cork man alone in Dublin, had been introduced to the Colleys by mutual friends. In the course

7

of a series of Sunday calls he had soon singled out my mother from the Mount Temple group of handsome, vivacious sisters. She was the unusual one—capricious, elusive, gently intent on her own thoughts. She and my father had in common a vagueness as to immediate things—so much so that her brothers and sisters wondered how she and he ever did arrive at anything so practical as an agreement to marry. They wondered, also, how Florence would keep house—and indeed she found this difficult at the start.

My father's and mother's families had in common the landowning Protestant outlook and Unionist politics. He and she, however, were individual people, departures from any family type. Tradition was, it is true, to be felt behind them, and in indifferent matters conditioned their point of view. But in matters in which they felt deeply they arrived at conclusions that were their own. True to their natures as man and woman, he was the more thoughtful, she the more feeling one. His mind had been formed by learning unknown to her: he lived by philosophy, she lived by temperament. His forehead, his talk, his preoccupations, were unmistakably those of an intellectual man, though a streak of young spontaneity in his nature redeemed him from stiffness or pedantry. As for her, because of her grace and vagueness, as well as her evident pleasure in the pretty and gay, she would not have been called an intellectual woman—for the bluestocking reigned as the type then. But she read and

8

she talked, and her thoughts were no less active for being half-submerged in her continuous dream.

Looking back, I see this—and see that my father and mother must have made by their marriage, and lived in, a world of their own. This world was seldom more than lightly impinged upon: times and happenings and the winter city of Dublin made round it a shadowy outer ring. Inside this world they each ruled their private kingdoms of thought, and inside it I, their first child, began to set up my own. My parents did not always communicate with each other, and I did not always communicate with them. They were both very independent of other people. I had been born, I see now, into a home at once unique and intensive, gently phenomenal. It may be because of this that my exterior memories of those winters in Dublin are so subjective, shifting, and unconcrete. I find myself writing now of visual rather than social memories. On the whole, it is things and places rather than people that detach themselves from the stuff of my dream.

My father, at the time when he fell in love with my mother, was a tall, shy, studious young man, loose-jointed and rather clumsy, with a head of springy, corn-coloured hair. He used to wear short whiskers down the sides of his cheeks—she soon persuaded him to have these off, and after that for some time he wore a moustache. I, however, remember him as a clean-shaven man.

NURSERY

MY HERBERT PLACE nursery, the first-floor drawing-room below it, and the dining-room under that, all had a watery quality in their lightness from the upcast reflections of the canal. The house was filled, at most daytime hours, by the singing hum of the sawmill across the water, and the smell of new-planed wood travelled across. Stacks of logs awaiting the saw over-topped the low tarred fence that ran along the bank on the opposite side. The wood-yard was fed from some of the barges that moved slowly up or down the canal, sinking into then rising again from locks. Not much wheeled traffic went past our door, but from each end of Herbert Place, intermittently, came the ring and rumble of trams going over bridges.

Herbert Place faced east: by midday the winter sun had passed from the front rooms, leaving them to grey-green reflections and their firelight, that brightened as dusk drew in.

My nursery reached across the breadth of the house; being high up, it had low windows, and bars had been fixed across these to keep me from falling out. On the blue-grey walls hung pictures, and two of these pictures I do remember sharply—they were openings into a second, more threatening reality. The

first must, I think, have been chosen for its heroic subject when my mother still expected me to be Robert: it
was Casabianca standing against the flames. The boy
stood in ecstasy on the burning deck. In the other, a
baby in a wooden cradle floated smilingly on an immense flood, stretching out its two hands to a guardian cat that sat upright on the quilt at the cradle's foot.
All round, from the lonely expanse of water rose only
the tips of gables, chimneys, and trees. The compo-
sure of the cat and the baby had been meant, I suppose, to rule all disaster out of the scene. But for me
there was constant anxiety—what would become of
the cradle in a world in which everyone else was
drowned? In fact, these two pictures induced in me a
secret suspended fear of disasters—fires and floods. I
feared to be cut off in high buildings, and the beautiful sound of rain was ruined for me by a certainty that
the waters must rise soon. Watching my moment, I
used to creep to a window to make sure that nothing
was happening yet. (When, later, I lived by the sea in
England, I was in equal dread of a tidal wave.) In no
other way was I a nervous child—and had my mother
guessed that the pictures would give me fancies she
would have certainly had them taken down.

Apart from the Casabianca, there to stimulate courage—for my father and mother, like all Anglo-Irish
people, saw courage apart from context, as an end in
itself—my nursery was planned to induce peace.
Peace streamed, it is true, from "The Herald Angels"
in their black-and-gold frame—a flight of angels

swept over a snowy landscape, casting light on the shepherds' upturned brows. And all around the nursery, under the pictures, ran a dado of nursery-rhyme scenes. I spied on its figures through the bars of my cot, and my mother taught me to know their names. She was free with the jingle of nursery rhymes, but reserved in the telling of fairy tales. She did not wish me, she said, to believe in fairies for fear that I might confuse them with angels. So, when I heard of fairies from other sources I thought of them as being trivial and flashy and (for some reason) always of German birth. Of Irish fairies I heard nothing at all. My mother's fears of confusion were quite baseless, for having seen pictures of both fairies and angels, I distinguished one from the other by the shape of their wings —fairies' wings were always of the butterfly type, while angels' had the shape and plumage of birds'. The smiling, sweeping, plumy presence of angels was suggested constantly to me—if I were to turn round quickly enough I might surprise my own Guardian behind me. My mother wished me to care for angels: I did.

I was content, however, not to intrude on angels by seeing one. I was content with what I could see already—the air round me not travelled by supernatural beings, only by birds. Dublin sparrows stayed for seconds together in jaunty flickering attitudes on my window bars. These were winter birds, ruffled up so plumply that they must wear extra feathers against the cold. (In the domain of summer, County Cork, I

12

learned to name singing birds, but sparrows were overlooked.) Another wintry distinction of Herbert Place was that gulls skimmed the canal and described flashes outside my window-panes. I heard they were driven inland by the storms that wrecked and twisted their own sea. "Poor gulls"—but they did not look it: alighting in twos and threes on the woodstacks they debonairly opened and shut their wings.

If I could see the Dublin quays as I must have seen them, I should remember more gulls. But between the Trinity College railings and the start of Sackville Street from the bridge there is an opaqueness or blank in my memory. Through a thinning of mist I just see the colonnades of the Bank of Ireland, that had been Our Own Parliament once. I never looked up Sackville Street without pleasure, for I was told it was the widest street in the world. Just as Phoenix Park, grey-green distance beyond the Zoo, was the largest park in the world. These superlatives pleased me almost too much: my earliest pride of race was attached to them. And my most endemic pride in my own country was, for some years, founded on a mistake: my failing to have a nice ear for vowel sounds, and the Anglo-Irish slurred, hurried way of speaking made me take the words "Ireland" and "island" to be synonymous. Thus, all other countries quite surrounded by water took (it appeared) their generic name from ours. It seemed fine to live in a country that was a prototype. England, for instance, was *"an* ireland" (or, a sub-Ireland)—an imitation. Then I learned that England was not even "an ireland," having failed to detach herself from the flanks of Scotland and Wales. Vaguely, as a Unionist child, I conceived that our politeness to England must be a form of pity.

In the same sense, I took Dublin to be the model of cities, of which there were imitations scattered over the world.

GOVERNESS

MY FIRST GOVERNESS, coming from England when I was four, must have been at pains to put this right. Before Miss Wallis I had had a nurse called Emma: she had a big broad face and I heard she was an Australian, but I hardly remember her at all. Before Emma, a nurse had been sent away in disgrace upon my mother's discovery that she doped me—she put "stuff" in my milk to keep me quiet. Perhaps that resourceful nurse unnaturally widened for me the infant sleep-zone: if so, she was less unkind than my mother believed. I may owe to her the slowness of my coming to consciousness—that consciousness that stores up intelligent memories. I seem to have fewer early memories than anybody with whom I have ever talked, so I must have stayed much later than other children inside the womb of a half-sleep. Like my bodily birth, the birth of my mind came late.

Miss Wallis, being a governess, stood for the element of intelligence. Her coming tore across some veil and first made me realize that I was I. Though, being a nursery-governess, she did not teach me, and went on performing for me the offices of a nurse. She did teach me one thing—towered over by her impatient patience I learned to button buttons and tie strings. To this independence of help in dressing some glory was supposed to attach. She continued, however, to put me into my gaiters, pinching my calves with each tweak of her buttonhook. And it was she who knotted then stuffed a cream silk handkerchief inside the collar of my outdoor coat. This odious preliminary to a walk in winter made it difficult for me to turn my head. I was not let out without this, or without gloves. The first coat that I remember was a dark-blue reefer—I was wearing this when I had the triumph of being called "Sonny" by a conductor who lifted me off a tram. My succeeding Dublin coats were of scarlet cloth. Sometimes I wore tam-o'-shanters. My hats were saucer-shaped, turning up all round over my hair, which I see now was very pretty—light gold, with the spring of a natural curl.

Miss Wallis, in her coiffure, face and body, was a composition of dinted and full curves. Puppy-fat still sheathed her nature: I know now she was not more than seventeen. This was her first post, and, impressed by herself and it, she overacted the gravity of an adult. Where I was concerned, her softness was tactile only: she did not love me. I remember questions I asked but remember nothing she said. She bored me and I bored her. Probably, like so many other young women, she slid through her hours in a narcissistic dream. But her contours make part of the Dublin contours in the first of my winters of memory. She was English—marvelling at us and at the scene without the wit that enjoys comparison—and she was my first governess. Those were the only two distinctions she had.

WALKS

ALONGSIDE this woman-girl, with her distillation of dullness, I took my week-day walks. (On Sundays I went out with my father and mother.) Either Miss Wallis's discretion or sentiments she must have been slowly forming governed the routes we took. It seems likely that we never walked on the quays—certain districts of Dublin being ruled out as "noisy"—and that we did not venture to cross the Liffey. So the North Side remained terra incognita. Yes, I do see the Four Courts, to which my father went every morning, and from which his black brief-bag with the thick red cord made its mysterious journeys home. Otherwise, painted with that one dome, the rest of the North Side was so much canvas on which had been contrived clouds and perspectives—smoke-and-slate-grey, brick-brown, and distance-blue. The canvas was pierced and entered only by the lordly perspective of Sackville Street. And till I went one day to a party in Mountjoy Square, I took it that Sackville Street had something queer at the end.

No swamp or jungle could hold more threats than the tacitly ruled-out parts of one's own city. Even along the verges of Stephen's Green there were canyonlike streets that could intimidate me. And the winter weather, in which I always knew it, went to make much of Dublin cryptic and austere, massed with those architectural shadows that make engravings frown. My fear was not social—not the rich child's dread of the slum. It was a charnel fear, of grave-dust and fungus dust. And it was claustrophobic—something might shut on me, never to let me out again; something might fall on me, never to let me through. I had heard of poverty-rotted houses that might at any moment crumble over one's head. Only on familiar pavements did sunshine fall.

My earliest beat was up and down the canal, from our front-door steps as far as Leeson Street Bridge. One joy, complete with the ingredient of terror, was to watch a barge go through a lock. The barge sank down intrepidly with the water into the sucking pit I was not allowed to approach. The gates could be felt straining. Then the barge slowly appeared again, with the black standing man on it still impassive, nothing further written upon his face. We would move along in admiration beside it as, negligently dragging its slow ripple, it now continued upon its way. We walked

17

on a level above the water and could look down on the
barge deck: between it and us ran a row of pollarded
trees.

My father had said the canal went to Limerick. Miss
Wallis, who cherished her few facts, was careful to tell
me this again. For "Limerick" I saw clotted patterns
of lace. "What's Limerick like?" I would ask her, anxious to get through the lace to some other reality. "I
don't know; I've never been there," replied Miss Wallis, without humiliation because she did not care. She
frustrated me with these negatives. Now it had begun
to wake up, my mind was restless with cravings; it
sought satisfactions it could not name or find. Intima-
tions of a world that I had been made for but apparently must not hope to possess were more troubling to
me, in those early winters, than anything that was to
come with my adolescence. I attempted to prey on
the people round me with questions and with my demands for stories and facts. Until I was seven—which
year saw, virtually, the close of my life in Dublin—I
was not allowed to learn to read: my mother believed
that reading would tire my eyes and brain. Actually,
frustrations tired me more. I was only allowed picture-
books. The pictures in these began to distend themselves, like those on the walls of my nursery and
round the dado, till they took on a momentous importance: they were my only clues to a mystery. And on
my walks through familiar quarters of Dublin I looked
at everything like a spy.

More alive than my walks alone with Miss Wallis

were my walks with the little Townshends, who lived
in Lansdowne Road, or with Vernie Cole. By chance,
almost all my parents' friends' children were boys.
There was Humphrey Fane Vernon, who taught me to
stand on my head, and whose home in Wilton Place I
passed almost daily: it had its flank turned to the canal. There was Noel Summers, who stayed at Clontarf Castle and wore his brown hair longer than mine.
The little Townshends, all male, were many; like me,
they all wore scarlet coats. I hoped people would take
them for my brothers; with them one had the sense of
trooping along. But Vernie Cole was my second
cousin, so I had a special lien with him. Sole and pre-
cocious child of brilliant parents—his father was a
professor, his mother (Cousin Blanche) a vivacious
blue-stocking—Vernie was a fount of ideas and facts.
He was small, thin, fair, pink-tipped, and energetic,
and always wore a fawn-coloured coat and cap. He
said, if I stepped on a tramline just after a tram had
passed I should be killed instantly by the electricity—
that electricity I could hear splutter along the wires
over my head. He also taught me words and phrases
in German. His *Fräulein*, walking behind with my
governess, would raise her voice now and then to con-
tradict what he said. . . . I connect Vernie, his information, and his pursuant *Fräulein* with the ample
front gardens, clean steps, and red window blinds of
the Waterloo Road. I think, though, that he walked
there rather than lived there. I cannot remember any
house where he lived.

19

The terrain across the canal from us looked open, compared to the city on our side. The houses were lower and either light grey or red. The streets were wider; the sheen of the spaced-out slate roofs seemed to reflect itself on the milky sky—sky in which the bells of the many churches dissolved without a fissure of city echo. There were gardens, half-moons of gravel, railings, and many trees. From the moment one had crossed the canal bridge it all had—I can see now—the spaciousness of a *banlieue*. The plan was still distinct, but it made for ease. None the less, this quarter was intersected by tramlines and hummed through by trams gathering speed.

Across here, one had a sense that the air lightened: the whole scene might have been the work of an artist with much white on his brush. Along the rows of big polished windows white lace curtains veiled the darkness of rooms. Bird-cages caught the sun on their bars, and statues, figures or white horses, stood in the fanlights over the doors.

I must say that in the "red roads" (such as Raglan Road) around St. Bartholomew's Church an expensive shadowy heaviness, and with it a sort of secrecy, increased. The large plum-red brick houses, with their porches and bow windows and gables, were mansions. They stood apart in lawns behind carriage gates, with evergreen bushes to screen them in. Here trams were quite out of hearing; the residential silence might be taken to be either null or rich. Between the mansions the roads ran almost empty, as though a premium

were set upon walking here. Evidently Miss Wallis—
in common with her successors—felt this: every English governess, in the red-road district, showed awe.
Between my mother's stylish contempt for the rich
people and my governesses' patent regard for money I
was divided and unsure which way to feel.

SHOPS

WE DID our everyday shopping in Upper Baggot
Street, just over the bridge. Here there was quite a
come-and-go in the mornings: you were in the Grafton Street of the trans-canal. Two rows of well-to-do
shops, each an irregular but unbroken frontage, faced
across at each other over the wide street. I most distinctly remember a chemist's, with the usual giant bottles of violet and green, a branch of Findlater's, a
baker's, a post-office (encaved at the back of a fancy
stationer's), and a draper's that yards of stuffs they
slung from up near the ceiling made as mysterious as a
Moorish tent. In this last shop they also sold china or-
naments—pink and gold princes and princesses with
blond gold-stippled hair. I bought a pair of these beings when I had been given a shilling for being good.

Soap, stamps, bunches of flowers, hat elastic for
me, all sorts of buttons but principally linen buttons,
picture post-cards, and things at the chemist's were

our most regular purchases. (For hats and coats and things that were more momentous we made the journey to the real Grafton Street.) As our cakes were made in the kitchen at Herbert Place, we were not regular customers at the cake-shop—though how dear to me was its spiced baking smell!

In our days in Upper Baggot Street everything was, in its way, classy: where white cotton coats were worn these were chalky clean, and sweet dry sawdust covered victuallers' floors. Everyone had not only manners but time; we nearby residents made this our own village. Unfamiliar faces seldom appeared; kind smiles came over the high counters at me, and almost everyone knew my name. A few red shops and a large red hospital had had places cut for them in the façades of grey. Through the swinging glass doors merchandise odours rolled to meet each other across the street: there was something embalmed and static even about the outdoor air. I do remember a wind that one day raced down the street, tugging the blue paper from the bunch of violets I held. And once, on the kerb outside Findlater's, a bit of grit blew into my eye.

Stretched across the roof lines of Upper Baggot Street I see a timeless white sky, a solution of sunshine in not imminent cloud—a sky for the favoured. Here I first knew the elation one gets from exchanging money for things. Between the kind rows of shops the in-and-out going traffic—for Baggot Street Bridge is one of the mouths of Dublin—seems to be checked by an unseen hand. The time mood of the street is half

22

past eleven of a February morning—half an hour before my morning rest. Except for the grit in my eye
I remember no contretemps except when I posted a
post-card not yet stamped— Yes, Miss Wallis once
bought herself a bottle of green scent, then dropped
and smashed it. A passing tram drowned her cry, but
her eyes crinkled for tears and the sub-adult mask
fell off her face. I understood, though without sympathy, that she was my age. Wetness crept through the
paper wrapping, and from the pavement violent
sweetness came up.

HORSE SHOW

As I CONTEMPLATE Upper Baggot Street, Miss Wallis's figure gives place almost imperceptibly (because
she was not important) to that of my second governess, Miss Baird, with whom I also went shopping here.
Miss Baird, both from coming a winter later in time
and from having more temperament, or, one might
say, more body, stands in my memory on a nearer
plane. Already experienced as a governess, she had
found means by which to deploy herself. She wore an
air of poetic languor, so that the performance of all
her duties seemed all the more a tribute to her sense of
the right. Her mode of dressing was at once *triste* and
smart—a little, I see now, that of a Frenchwoman. I

23

recall her dark fluffy hair and intense long-lashed eyes. She had wit enough to avoid the emotional boredom attendant on her rather lonely position by creating an emotional tie with me: she kept me tuned in to her moods, which were variable. While Miss Wallis had looked at Ireland with a stodgy wonder, Miss Baird, in her disliking or liking, vibrated a little to all she saw. I began to perceive, in her company, that Ireland was not the norm, the usual thing.

With Miss Baird my walks were longer. We not only crossed the canal but crossed the Dodder, though I still do not think that we crossed the Liffey. Quite often we went as far as Ballsbridge. As a child of a member of the Royal Dublin Society, I had permission to enter the Show buildings, penetrate glass-topped halls and ironbound passages, and scale the empty grandstands above the oval of green. More interesting than a mountainside from being artificial, each grand-stand gradated into the high-up darkness under its roof. Over all this, that I grew up to call the Horse Show, in these winter months a towering silence reigned. For mornings together we met no one; we heard only the echoes we raised. The void and the echoes were theatrical: stranger for being exposed to daylight, this was the first empty theatre that I saw. Looking down from the top of a grandstand, I found the ideal answer to the child's wish to be monarch of everything. Proud and a little giddy, I looked down. My governess remained glued to the bottom, watching phantom horses go round and round.

Our rule of County Cork summers—in which months, as I have said, Dublin seemed to be rolled up and put away—made the real August feast of Horse Show less than nothing to me. My father (out of some lingering opposition to *his* father, who was a hard rider) was bored by horses; my mother really disliked them. If our County Cork neighbours journeyed up for the Horse Show, it was not of it that we spoke when they came back. We were, I suppose, in Dublin during the Spring Show, but my father and mother ignored that. So, until I was grown up, the acres of Ballsbridge buildings seemed to dedicate emptiness to a sounding name.

On our way out, I chased myself round the cast-iron pillars and swung on the unlocked turnstiles in winter light diffused by a glare of glass.

I connect the Ballsbridge grandstands with the Russo-Japanese War. It had been made known to me that war had, that year, escaped from the locked strong-room of history into the present—though this was happening, as it *could* only happen, at the unsafe other side of the world. I knew of Russians as fur-clad people who drove in sledges pursued by wolves; I knew of the Japanese as the prototype of my Aunt Laura's tonsured, lackadaisical doll that had a sash gummed to its middle and sleeves of paper gummed to its flapping arms. From Japan came the crinkled lanterns, the parasols, and the little miracle discs, as small as pills, that in water uncurled into lovely blooms. For me the Japanese had made these, with the smiles of artists and patient hands. How sure it was, in those days, that still unnamed propaganda of prettiness! In common with most of England and Anglo-Ireland, I was pro-Japanese.

Hearing a clock strike, one morning, with more meaning than usual, I stopped halfway up a grandstand to realize that time held war. The hour was more than my hour; within it people were fighting; the fur and the paper people grimaced with hate at each other and let off guns. This was happening—happening as surely as I raised my right foot to put it on a new tier. This was my first vision—I mean, the first moment in which I conceived of reality as being elsewhere than in me. . . . Twelve having struck, my governess looked round. It was time for me (again) to go home and rest.

My rests—in the hour preceding midday dinner, in the curtain-darkened Herbert Place front room—were my high points of restlessness. In these I most felt the vacuum, the hunger-pain, set up in me from being unable to read. Nothing would make me a daytime sleeper. My eyes went gimletting through the unnatural dusk, into the pictures, into the nursery-rhyme groups round the dado, trying to force action on what I saw. The trams on the bridges loudened. Even in our quiet quarter the city sounds of Dublin, at this hour, rose to a climax—a climax from which I was withheld. The energies that my rests were supposed to store up used this hour to burn themselves out in.

STEPHEN'S GREEN

YES, for quiet walking we crossed the canal. But Dublin, the city behind Herbert Place, was magnetic. Miss Baird liked centres of life; she liked Grafton Street; she liked Stephen's Green with its patterns of lawns and lake, its peopled footbridge, its mounds and its boskage that was romantic even in wintertime. Though English, she was born Continental; the most nearly foreign governess that I had. She could divine (in the water-divining sense) any possible scene of fashion. Often, and not really I think from kindness, we went out to feed the ducks in Stephen's Green. I carried the bag of crusts; she carried a muff. Towards the point where we took up our station, on the kerb of the lake, the water-fowl converged with a darting smoothness, their ripples making spokes of a fan.

Among the floating and bloating crusts the reflections were broken up. The birds jabbed brutally with their beaks. I tried to insist on justice: there was always a slow duck or a wistful duck that did not get anything. Round me and the lake the rock-stuck mounds and the arbour-work against the evergreens sometimes glittered or glistened in sunshine that was frosty or damp, but were sometimes haunted or derelict under a brown veil. The lake's polish varied with our days. Under my nostrils the smell of sopping

27

bread filled the air. The trams running round us, outside the trees and railings, according to weather sounded distant or near. The throbbing tune of a barrel-organ underran the hum and rumble of traffic: for minutes together a tune took command of the city. Everyone seemed to listen; it seemed to suspend the world.

At one of these minutes I remember my mother standing on the bridge over the lake, looking for us. She sometimes came here on an impulse to join Miss Baird and me. Her hat was perched on the hair piled over her pointed face; I could have known her only by the turn of her head as she looked along the lake for my scarlet coat. I was as easy to see as a pillar-box. She started toward us through the strolling and standing people as though through a garden that was her own.

My mother's feeling for Stephen's Green was native, subtle, nostalgic, unlike Miss Baird's. As a young girl between classes at Alexandra College, she had walked and sat here—sometimes in love with a person, always in love with an idea. The most intense moments of her existence all through her life had been solitary. She often moved some way away from things and people she loved, as though to convince herself that they did exist. Perhaps she never did quite convince herself, for about her caresses and ways with me I remember a sort of rapture of incredulity. Her only child had been born after nine years of waiting—and even I was able to understand that she did not take me or

her motherhood for granted. She was so much deso-
lated that she unnerved me when anything went
wrong between her and me. If my mother was a per-
fectionist, she had the kind of wisdom that goes with
that make-up. She explained to me candidly that she
kept a governess because she did not want to scold me
herself. To have had to keep saying "Do this," "Don't
do that," and "No," to me would have been, as she
saw it, a peril to everything. So, to interpose between
my mother and me, to prevent our spending the best
part of our days together, was the curious function of
every governess. It was not that there were more
pressing claims on my mother's time: she was not a
worldly woman (though she did like pleasure) and
my father was out the greater part of the day. When
she was not with me she thought of me constantly,
and planned ways in which we could meet and could
be alone.

I know now the feeling with which she stood on the
bridge, looked along the lake till she came to my
scarlet coat, then thought: "That is my child!"

When I had been born my mother was thirty-four
—so that in these winters I write about she was approaching the end of her thirties. I do not remember
her clothes distinctly; I only see the fluid outline of
her. I believe that she had a sealskin jacket and that
her skirts swept barely clear of the ground. One of my
father's brothers sent back from South Africa grey
ostrich feathers for her and white for me. She possessed an ermine wrap and a string of pearls, and dia-

mond and other rings that she wore on her blue-veined hands. Her style of dressing was personal; a touch of haughtiness set her against fashion. Susceptible to her charm, the glow of her face and being, I could feel its action on people round us—of this she was never conscious herself. She could withdraw into such a complete abstraction that she appeared to enter another world. Her beauty—for I know now it was beauty—was too elusive and fine for a child to appreciate: I thought I only thought she was lovely because I loved her.

She wore her bronze-coloured hair (which was threaded with silver early) in a pompadour over her forehead; at the back the hair was brushed up from the nape of her neck, then coiled on the top of her head. She shored up the weight of it with curved tortoise-shell combs. Her eyes, alternately pensive and quizzical, were triangular, with arched upper lids; they were of a grey-blue that deepened, and she had large pupils. Her dark eyebrows were expressive. When she smiled her nose turned down at the tip, and the smile sent her cheeks up in subtle curves. In her cheeks showed the blue-pink of a sweet-pea. She flushed easily, when she was startled or angry, drank red wine, or sat too near a fire—for this last reason there were hand-screens, of stretched silk painted with flowers, all over the drawing-room at Herbert Place. Her complexion had the downy bloom of a peach, and she dusted this over with fuller's earth. She used *Peau d'Espagne* scent. Her name, Florence, suited her.

BRASS PLATES

BETWEEN the middle of Dublin and Herbert Place
lies a tract of Georgian streets and squares. We had a
choice of two routes into the city. From the foot of our
steps we could turn right, then go along Lower Baggot Street; or we could turn left, take the curve round
St. Stephen's Church, and after that go along Upper
Mount Street and the south side of Merrion Square;
to this route was added the charm of going through
Leinster Lawn, between the Museum and the National Gallery; one then followed that secretive passage, under the high flank of Leinster House, through
to the circular lawn on the other side and the gates
opening onto Kildare Street.

(When I was with my father, the glory of the Royal
Dublin Society was upon us and we took the indoor
short cut, through the Leinster House rooms.)

The perspectives of this quarter of Dublin are to
any eye, at any time, very long. In those first winters
they were endless to me. The tense distances that one
only slowly demolished gave a feeling of undertaking
to any walk. Everything in this quarter seemed out-
size. The width of the streets, the stretch of the
squares, the unbroken cliff-like height of the houses,
made the human idea look to me superhuman. And

31

there was something abstract about this idea, with its built-up planes of shadow and light.

At the same time, the complexion of these façades humanly altered from day to day. The neighbourhood seemed infused with a temper or temperament of its own, and my spirits, on morning or afternoon walks, corresponded with this in their rise and fall. . . . Some days, a pinkish sun-charged gauze hung even over the houses that were in shadow; sunlight marked with its blades the intersections of streets and dissolved over the mews that I saw through archways. On such days, Dublin appeared to seal up sunshine as an unopened orange seals up juice. The most implacable buildings were lanced with light; the glass half-moons over the darkest front doors glowed with sun that, let in by a staircase window, fell like a cascade down flights of stairs.

But as often I felt a malign temper at work. Stories of gloom would add themselves to the houses, till these shut out the sky. The streets tautened and the distances frowned. Walking down Upper Mount Street or Lower Baggot Street, I at once had the feeling of being in the wrong, and Leeson Street became a definite threat. Any human movement about the pavements showed signs of infection by nervous moodiness. But there never was much movement: though I took this for granted (as being the rule of cities) I saw too few people in view of the height and space. The tyrannical grandness of this quarter seemed to exist for itself alone. Perhaps a child smells history without knowing it—I did not know I looked at the tomb of fashion.

Even so, this quarter had declined, since the Union, to nothing worse than a sombre, solid propriety. This was not really a case of bare ruined choirs. The houses in which my Anglo-Irish progenitors, gathering round their Parliament, had made merry with a stylish half-savagery were the homes of professional people now. I know now it did mark the end of an epoch when the first brass plate appeared in Merrion Square. The original lordly plan had been dedicated to Society; it commemorated the migration southwards across the river after the Duke of Leinster had taken his bold decision to sink the foundations of his great new house in a snipe bog. The original is never alone for long, and Society took chances after the Duke.

The post-Union exodus of the bright-plumaged people had not (as I saw) been followed by real decay. The Irish Bar and the eminent Dublin doctors kept South Dublin witty and sociable. Judges and specialists now lived round Merrion Square. The front doors were painted, the fanlights and windows polished, the great staircase possibly better swept, and the high-ceilinged double drawing-rooms heated and lit for *conversazioni*. In the winters of my childhood this second society was still in full, if not at its fullest, force. The twentieth century governed only in name; the nineteenth was still a powerful dowager. Between England and Anglo-Ireland a time-lag is, I think, always perceptible. Any transition into Edwardian dashingness would have been seen in the Castle set. But the Castle seasons left my father and mother cold. The world my parents inhabited, and the sub-world of its children, was still late Victorian. Their friends were drawn from the Bar, from Trinity College, from among the prelates of the Church of Ireland or landed people quietly living in town.

In fact, the climatic moodiness of South Dublin (a bold Italianate town-plan in tricky Celtic light) must have existed only in my eye. All here stood for stability. The front doors were, as I say, fresh-painted—crimson, chocolate, chestnut, ink-blue, or olive-green. One barrister friend of my father's had a chalk-white front door I found beautiful. And each door—to this my memory finds no single exception—bore its polished brass plate. Daughter of a professional neighbourhood, I took this brass plate announcing its owner's name to be the *sine qua non* of any gentleman's house. Just as the tombstone says "Here Lies," the plate on the front door (in my view) said "Here Lives." Failure to write one's name on one's door seemed to me the admission of nonentity. The householder with the anonymous door must resign himself to being overlooked by the world—to being passed by by the postman, unfed by tradesmen, guestless, unsought by friends—and his family dwelt in the shadow of this disgrace.

The fact that I could not read made these plates with writing still more significant. The first time I did see a town front door of unmistakable standing *without* a plate, I remember being not only scornful but hostile. Why should the dweller here envelop himself in mystery? On that occasion, my mother explained to me that plates were not, after all, the rule. If not, why not? I said hotly: how very silly. How else was one to know who lived in a house? In the light of this fixed idea (which I still think a good one) I remember my first view of London—street after street of *triste* anonymity. So no one cares who lives in London, I thought. No wonder London is so large; all the non-entities settle here. Dublin has chosen to be smaller than London because she is grander and more exclusive. All the important people live in Dublin, near me.

At the top of the Herbert Place front steps, waiting for the front door to be opened (for my governess never carried a latchkey), I would trace with my finger my father's name. This was not an act of filial piety only; it gave him an objective reality, which I shared.

DANCING IN DAYLIGHT

THE CHILDREN I met at dancing class bore the surnames inscribed on those brass plates. There were a few who came from further away, from the red roads the far side of the canal. These made their longer journey to Molesworth Street by tram, or, on bad days, even in cabs. And there were, in addition, one or two pupils whose addresses and background mystery veiled: possibly they may have been Roman Catholics; I never knew more of them than their Christian names. Children whom I met nowhere else could not but be magnetic to the imagination. They appeared to share some secret among themselves—if only the secret of being unknown to me.

These weekly classes of Miss Thieler's took place in the late morning, or early afternoon. Only as a pupil is one to know the sensation of ballroom dancing in sunshine. Long dusty dazzling shafts slanted onto us through the pointed windows of the Molesworth Hall. The sun was made theatrical and unlikely by the pertinacious drumming of the piano. One twirled in and out of it, half-blinded; it heightened the prim abandon of the barn dance, the giddiness of the waltz. The dust, I suppose, was raised by our dancing feet; where it can have come from I cannot think, for the smell of the Molesworth Hall was of scrubbed floors. It had a Protestant smell. The hall, approached by a flight of twisted stone stairs, is Gothic. The high pitch of its roof and its high-up windows give it a decidedly churchlike air. And so sunk was the floor in its surround of chocolate dado that one might have been dancing on the floor of a well.

On benches placed round against the dado, or (if not too shy) on the platform at the end of the room, the mothers, nurses, and governesses took their seats. They had had first to peel off from us the many wrappings in which little girls braved the weather on the way to Miss Thieler's. Over our shivery muslins, under our topcoats, would be several jerseys and a tied-across shawl. Thick stockings went over openwork stockings, and often gaiters were buttoned on top of this. In those days, everybody subscribed to the idea that children were perishable. Even little boys arrived in a mobled state. In fact, South Dublin children bound for Miss Thieler's were to be recognized by their abnormal size.

Yet I do not remember ever setting out on a really cold day. Once or twice I remember mornings so dark that Miss Thieler ordered the gas-jets to be lit. Once, fog rolled after us into the Molesworth Hall. How or whether the hall was heated I do not know. . . . Our hair was given a final brushing and our dancing sandals snapped onto our feet. At last we shook out our muslins and took the floor—gingerly, like bathers entering chilly water. The pianist struck experimentary chords, just like an orchestra tuning up, while Miss Thieler, talking away to someone, appraised us out of the corner of her eye.

She was by birth (I think) an Austrian—petite, dark, elegant, ageless, with rather pronounced features and the not very happy vitality of a flame, that quivers and tears at the air uneasily, wanting to devour more than it can. Like a flame, she was surrounded by a vibration, wherever she moved. Her face reflected the rhythm of every dance we went through, and we could see her suffer when we murdered the rhythm. As a teacher she was an artist: she was probably the first artist I knew.

Because I had heard she was Continental—or came, at least, of a Continental family—I differentiated her foreignness from the less pure, inferior foreignness of my English governess. I do not know what her feelings of race were. I do not know what she thought of us Anglo-Irish children, from whom the austere grace of one race had been bred away and who still missed the naïve, positive gracelessness of another. I would say that, in general, the Anglo-Irish do not make good dancers; they are too spritely and conscious; they are incapable of one kind of trance or of being sensuously impersonal. And, for the formal, pure dance they lack the formality: about their stylishness (for they have stylishness) there is something impromptu, slightly disorderly. As pupils one saw what she thought of us—she opened the class in a mood of neutral, warning patience; if we slacked or blundered, her tongue could be a lash; she had one degree of half-praise, an ironic surprise that was very stimulating. When, by some felicity, one broke through for a minute into pure dancing she would by a half-involuntary look salute one—for that minute one was the equal of her.

Just as she never spared us, she never flattered our mothers or keepers seated around the walls. And this, in the part of our city where we were constantly flattered, did more than anything to exalt her—what a famous dancing-teacher she was! Happy (but rare) the mother who could go home saying: "Miss Thieler was pleased today with my little girl."

As we trickled into our places across the floor, we little girls as white as the ballerinas of Swan Lake, but with the action of clumsy cygnets, I suppose we all felt (I felt certainly) that something psychic inside each child or the day had already determined whether that child, today, should be a duffer or able to dance.

I was a crack polka-dancer, springing around the floor: I had been taught that step in the drawing-room at home. Unhappily, the jerkiness of the polka infected everything else I tried—for weeks together I could not learn to waltz. I was not even allowed to take a partner, but, for interims that held up the entire class, had to go round the floor in a single file of duffers while Miss Thieler, head fallen wearily sideways, beat the pads of her hands together—"One two *three*, four five *six!*"—at each turn of a bar and end of a bar. The piano, meanwhile, with an insulting loud slowness played.

This was dreadful. She kept us duffers in such *tenue* that I dared not even hold my head forward to let my hair flop curtains over my burning cheeks. A feeling of doom and of inability was drawn tight like a wire noose round my brain. Then, one morning, at the dreadful height of such minutes, a spring released itself in my inside. My feet and body released themselves, without warning, from inside the noose of my consciousness. Like a butterfly free of the chrysalis, like a soul soaring out of the body, I burst from the file of duffers and went spinning smoothly, liquidly round the floor by myself. I waltzed. The piano dropped its disdainful note and quickened and melted in sympathy. I felt no floor under my feet: this was my dream of being able to fly. I *could* fly—I could waltz. So much the sun of heaven was in my eyes that I saw nothing. All round me surprise, and something more than surprise, created a sort of unheard cheer. Though I was a vain child I felt no pride: the experience was too pure. Like a top from a lick of the magic whip, I spun on and on in my course, till I slowed, staggered, was giddy, and flopped down.

"So you've managed to learn to waltz," my governess said as we walked home. "I thought you could, if you tried." (How little she knew.) "You must hurry and tell your mother; she *will* be pleased."

"You tell her—I'd rather you did," I said.

White muslin was, as I say, *de rigueur* for Miss Thieler's. In the bars of sunshine it lit up, and its very flimsiness looked gay. Its inappropriateness to a winter morning, and to the Gothic height, matt plaster, and harsh scrubbed boards of the Molesworth Hall, gave it a perverse chic. On a glassy floor, between mirrors, under lit chandeliers, we might have looked the tame little things we were. I was allowed a white satin bow to my top-knot, and an Indian silver bangle on each wrist. By some unwritten law of our time and class, no child might be dressed as though she meant to excel. At Miss Thieler's, the few transgressors of this law were objects of endless envy to me. There were always two or three little girls who wore dresses of accordion-pleated ivory silk, and whose openwork stockings and dancing sandals were bronze instead of black. But outstanding, because it was so illicit, was the beauty of Mavis and Paula G——. Their hair was the blond that is called platinum now; their accordion-pleated dresses were light leaf-green and they wore scarlet stockings and shoes. To top this, they were beautiful dancers, blowing about the floor like parrot feathers, like petals on a light wind.

Some penalty is said to attach to beauty. In the case of Mavis and Paula nothing, in those winters, had shown its hand. I am not even sure they were Roman Catholics. I wonder what became of them: possibly they died young. The worst I ever heard said of them was that they were not, somehow, quite like the rest at Miss Thieler's dancing class.

Among the few boys, my favourite partner was Fergus. Under the influence of this daylight dancing my relations with him were at least faintly romantic, as my relations with Vernie and the little Townshends were not. He had a burnished red head and wore an Eton suit, but his great charm, in my eyes, was his maturity—he must have been at least nine or ten. If he did not seek me out, I sought him. But, with implacable male snobbishness—a snobbishness I should be sorry to see decline—he did not make even this possible until the morning when I had learned to waltz. He was a smooth, if stocky, waltzer himself. I cannot remember a word he said, and in repose his face went a little wooden, but I suppose that, apart from his age, I liked him because he was a man of the world.

SOCIETY

ONE WINTER, Miss Thieler gave a sort of gala or exhibition at the Rathmines Town Hall. She held several classes besides the one I attended, and she assembled the pick of her pupils here. To have been bidden was an elating thing. The time was late afternoon; we drove up in cabs; down the Rathmines Road lay sunset on frosty mist. Inside my casing of shawls I was rigid with nervousness, for I was to take part in two dances upon the platform—a sort of elaboration of Pat-a-Cake and the miming of Ten Little Nigger Boys. We had summoned this very rare cab because my mother—in common, I found later, with several other mothers—did not know how to find Rathmines Town Hall. She was accompanying Miss Baird and me because she was so proud of my being "chosen." She shared my nervousness, which she made worse. On that afternoon I saw the point of her policy of keeping Miss Baird between us as a non-conductor, chaperon, buffer state.

Fergus was too big and too grand to be expected to

caper upon a platform, but was there that day as a specimen waltzing man, and at least twice I was chosen to partner him. I remember not much more about that afternoon, because the heat and lights of the Rathmines Town Hall dissolve the scene, till it runs together with many other parties to which I went. These parties, unlike Miss Thieler's, had no object but pleasure: they were in no way dedicated to art. They were from half past four to seven or eight o'clock; the guests were children not yet into their teens.

Most of the well-to-do houses of South Dublin entertained for their children round Christmas-time. Quite often, one's cab crossed the canal, for the spreading mansions along the red roads, with their frosty gardens and steamy conservatories, vied with the cliff-like blocks round Merrion Square. Even houses I knew well became, on these occasions, unfamiliar and heatedly large and light. The front door opened upon the roar of coal fires burning in every festive room. One met portieres looped back, white paint dazzling in gaslight that poured through crimped pink glass shades, flowers banked up out of harm's way, fur rugs expectantly rolled back and big chintz sofas in retreat against the walls. The pent-up silence in which children assemble, a rustle of fidgeting (like the wind in corn), could be heard as one was led past the drawing-room door to lay off one's coat and shawls in a room above.

The day of any one of these parties always dawned

with a particular hue. I was often unable to eat my dinner; my throat would be tense and my heart bumped. My excited state being recognized, I was compelled to rest for an extra hour—and, each phase of pre-party ritual being hallowed, I could extract pleasure even from this. Not long after half past three they began to dress me, in the humid afternoon twilight of Herbert Place: each garment was aired behind the guard of the nursery fire and gave out a sweet warmed smell. At stages during the dressing I would break free for solemn jumping about. For parties I was allowed to wear jewellery; a heart-shaped locket on a gold chain or a shamrock brooch with a pearl impaled upon it.

I believe a child's view of a party to be purer than the grown-up view—more classic, impersonal. Ideas of personal display or of romantic encounter are equally absent from its mind. I mean, a child goes to a party without motive; it does not hope to show off or to fall in love. The ulterior designs of the marriage market are absent from parties given for children of young age; the personality show of the "intellectual" party is a thing not, happily, yet in view. To the hostess is attributed royal kindness, of which there can be no thought of return. And the fellow-guests, the children, are metamorphosed: in their lacy dresses or dark suits they are the beau monde. You may have often met them; you may have known them; you may have pulled their hair. Or they may be strangers: it is different. In the hot, lit, packed room full of beating hearts, with its psychic orchestra soundlessly tuning up, everything is subsidiary to "the party." Little girls go in groups to show each other their lockets; little boys study their own feet. But the self is dissolved. You see children looking shyly into the mirrors to convince themselves of their own reality.

I pity people who do not care for Society: they are poorer for the oblation they do not make.

In the Anglo-Irish children of my time, shyness was regarded as a deformity. A mother whose child could not face a party blushed. We were brought up to be pleasing grown-up people, and it was taken that we could contend with each other. This, as the evening went on, we no doubt did. The ice dome broke—only too soon, for with it went that certain ineffability. The party became like a cut cake. And many cakes—pink and white and chocolate—*were* soon cut, in the course of dining-room tea. We continued to eat with a mounting clatter, without the inanities of talk. Our jaws and stomachs had functioned before our ordinary senses returned to life. Ladies with silver dishes and cups of tea inclined their busts between the backs of our chairs. Scarlet and orange crackers would be stacked down the table, round the vases of holly and hothouse flowers, round the *bonbonnières,* round the cakes, and the moment when these crackers were to be pulled, approaching, ruined for many of us the end of tea. I was not the only child present who was cracker-shy, but I might be the only child too vain to show that I was. A number of little girls enacted their fear so prettily that I doubted that it could be real at all: they folded up on themselves with their hands spread over their ears and their elbows digging into their sashes, or went through the motions of diving under the table. I once saw a little boy who suffered what I suffered: leaning right back, in his velvet suit, he was going slowly green in the face. . . . At one terrible party we were expected to take part in a cracker-pulling grand chain—you crossed hands, as for Auld Lang Syne, and all pulled at once.

In the air hot with gunpowder and excited cries I could glean spoils from the crackers I had not pulled. Having made a quick collection of scraps and tinsel, I traded these for trinkets and paper caps.

At the best parties, I mean the grandest parties, dancing alternated with musical games. Ladies succeeded each other at the piano, which was seldom silent except in the crashing pauses of Musical Chairs and during the sort of cabaret—magic lantern, Santa Claus, shadow-play, funny man—by which, by tradition, the evening was cut in two. Once or twice I remember a Christmas tree. At the Fane Vernons' I ate my first strawberry ice. I also remember, in connection with this party, my first real disconcerting sight of myself. Importantly holding the fluted glass ice-plate, I moved opposite myself in a full-length mirror, in order to give the moment double effect. But the mouthful of ice froze to my palate as I saw how right my mother had been: my dress, the dress I had insisted on wearing, did not become me. It had lately arrived

46

from London, the Christmas present of an English cousin as kind as she was rich—it was of ivory satin scalloped with ecru lace. When my mother called the dress "hard" I had not believed her—I took this as one more manifestation of her too derisive attitude towards wealth. Now, opposite the glare of the Fane Vernons' mirror, with children milling behind me, I abjured my mistake. Above the ornate white satin collar I saw my face harsh and brick-pink, my top-knot an iron whorl. The dress had done to my being what the ice was doing to my inside. . . . For years I would not eat an ice again.

SUNDAYS

ON SUNDAYS we went to St. Stephen's, our parish church, a few minutes' walk along the canal. St. Stephen's Georgian façade, with its pillars and steps, crowns the Upper Mount Street perspective, and looks down it into the airy distance of Merrion Square. To the ascending sound of bells we went up the steps— my mother with a fine-meshed veil drawn over her features, my father already removing his top hat, I in my white coat. The Sunday had opened with mysterious movements about the staircase of Herbert Place— my mother and father's departure to "early church."

About this Matins *I* went to there was no mystery. I

could be aware that this was only an outer court. None the less, I must not talk or look behind me or fidget, and I must attempt to think about God. The church, heart of and key to this Protestant quarter, was now, at mid-morning, packed: crosswise above the pews allotted to each worshipping family ran galleries, with, I suppose, more people up there. The round-topped windows let in on us wintry, varying, but always unmistakably Sunday light, and gas burned where day did not penetrate far enough. The interior, with its clear sombreness, sane proportions, polished woodwork and brasswork, and aisles upon which confident feet rang, had authority—here one could feel a Presence were it only the presence of an idea. It emphasized what was at once august and rational in man's relations with God. Nowhere was there any intensity of darkness, nowhere the point of a small flame. There was an honourable frankness in the tone in which we rolled out the General Confession—indeed, sin was most felt by me, in St. Stephen's, as any divagation from the social idea. There was an ample confidence in the singing, borne up by the organ's controlled swell.

Bookless (because I could not read), I mouthed my way through the verse of hymns I knew. Standing packed among the towering bodies, I enjoyed the feeling that something was going on. During the prayers I kneeled balanced on two hassocks, and secretly bit, like a puppy sharpening its teeth, into the waxed prayer-book ledge of our pew. Though my inner ear was already quick and suspicious, I detected, in the course of that morning service, no hypocritical or untrue note. If I did nothing more, I conformed. I only did not care for the Psalms, which struck me as savage, discordant, complaining—or, sometimes, boastful. They outraged all the manners I had been taught, and I did not care for this chanted airing of troubles.

My mother attended St. Stephen's out of respect for my father's feeling that one should not depart from one's parish church. He mistrusted, in religion as in other matters, behaviour that was at all erratic or moody; he had a philosophic feeling for observance and form. But she liked St. Bartholomew's better because it was "higher," and once or twice in the course of every winter she would escape and take me there. Archbishop Trench and his daughters were her cousins; the happiest days of her girlhood had been spent at the Palace, and for the rest of her days she remained High Church. She spoke of "Prods" (or extreme, unctuous Protestants) with a flighty detachment that might have offended many. I was taught to say "Church of Ireland," not "Protestant," and "Roman Catholic," not simply "Catholic."

It was not until after the end of those seven winters that I understood that we Protestants were a minority, and that the unquestioned rules of our being came, in fact, from the closeness of a minority world. Roman Catholics were spoken of by my father and mother with a courteous detachment that gave them, even, no myth. I took the existence of Roman Catholics for granted but met few and was not interested in them. They were, simply, "the others," whose world lay alongside ours but never touched. As to the difference between the two religions, I was too discreet to ask questions—if I wanted to know. This appeared to share a delicate, awkward aura with those two other differences—of sex, of class. So quickly, in a child's mind, does prudery seed itself and make growth that I remember, even, an almost sexual shyness on the subject of Roman Catholics. I walked with hurried step and averted cheek past porticos of churches that were "not ours," uncomfortably registering in my nostrils the pungent, unlikely smell that came round curtains, through swinging doors. On Sundays, the sounds of the bells of all kinds of churches rolled in a sort of unison round the Dublin sky, and the currents of people quitting their homes to worship seemed to be made alike by one human habit, such as of going to dinner. But on week-days the "other" bells, with their (to my ear) alien, searching insistence, had the sky and the Dublin echoes all to themselves. This predisposition to frequent prayer bespoke, to me, some incontinence of the soul.

In the afternoons of Sunday, St. Stephen's held Children's Service. The specialness of the service, and its formula, was flattering to my infant state. God might show grown-up preference for the grown-up people, but we children had our lien—conspiracy, almost—with Christ Jesus. Toy Service Sunday was the crown of my Christian year. On this day, each child carried with it to church a toy, to be blessed by Jesus, then sent to poor children in hospitals. Ideally, you brought what you valued most; in fact, it was hard to avoid the idea of show—for how narrowly we eyed each other's oblations! At a signal, we all filed out of our pews, to carry our toys up to the communion rails. This was the one approach to the altar that, as Protestant children, we were for years to make. And, these toys having shared our intimate lives, this was the nearest to a sacrament that we came. I remember carrying up a large woolly dog; it was life-sized, had a buoyant spring to its tail, and barked when you pulled the wire under its chin.

The dog had been, perhaps two winters ago, a completely surprising gift to me from two Colley uncles at Mount Temple. So long as my mother's mother lived, we had spent at her house almost every winter Sunday afternoon. These expeditions to Clontarf, on which we set out not long after midday dinner, involved a tram ride across Dublin (including the eventful change at the Pillar) and an emergence from the North Side into view of the sea and the Bay's glistening flats of mud. I believed, for I had been reared on mythology, that the tract called the Bull had been christened after Europa's friend.

At the corner where we got off for Mount Temple, I remember the smell of the wintry evergreens mingled with a stagnant smell of the sea. At this corner, one Sunday, without warning, I set up a hullabaloo. I thought I had left my white muff on the tram—the

tram that was now resuming its way to Howth. My
father, who was a clumsy runner, gave chase and
made imploring signals in vain. My mother, kneeling
to throw her arms around me, simultaneously suffered
with him and me. I then broke off my howling— I
had located my muff. Worn round my neck on a white
silk cord, it had "travelled": it now hung safely behind
my back. Now quite calm, I could observe with surprise the repercussion of all this on my parents. It was
typical, I suppose, of the three of us that we should
have forgotten I wore my muff on a cord.

Though Mount Temple had ended before I was
five years old, I must have been old enough, in its
day, to idealize, for I remember that house as being
under a magic glass. A short but powerful avenue
served to cut it off from the residential roads. Trees
massed the carriage sweep on the north side, but the
large windows of the double drawing-room looked out
down open lawns pale with winter, and held, till well
after tea-time, the last of the light from the lawns and
sea. Many low late Victorian chairs, tables, and sofas
were disposed about, in the heat of the roaring fire.
From the chairs and sofas and from the window-
seats rose up smilingly, as we entered, uncles and
aunts. Down a flight of staircase or through an arch-
way rang the rallying voice of my grandmother. She
was a woman, I can suppose now, with rather too
much energy to her charm. She loved me—perhaps as
a kind of atonement, for she had not got on very well
with my mother. I enjoyed and admired her more than

I loved her. I loved Aunt Laura, who almost immediately took me up to her bedroom to continue my
friendship with Thomas, her Japanese doll. And Aunt
Maud was a notable story-teller who continued, each
Sunday, our own private serial.

My uncles, who came and went, were handsome,
easy, and kind. My mother, I believe, was their favourite sister. It was like my uncles to give me that
life-sized dog without comment and for no reason at
all—I mean, it was not Christmas. The dog was simply standing under a table, turning to the fire its glass
eyes. They allowed me to pat it silently, for an interval
in which all my desires had time to mount. Then
they said: "It's for you." . . . I may say that in real
life I was not very fond of animals. I would not have
wished to change this for a "real" dog.

DRAWING-ROOM

AFTER Mount Temple came to an end, the Sunday-
evening illusion of perfection transferred itself to our
own drawing-room at Herbert Place. The younger
Mount Temple faces reappeared here. Those days, I
was old enough, and long-legged enough, to join my
father on his afternoon Sunday walks—sometimes towards the Dodder-bank country, sometimes towards
the Sandymount sea. Coming in, he and I seldom

found my mother alone. Uncle George Colley, for instance, now lodged only three doors from us, in Herbert Place, and when he was not out driving his red motor-car he was generally with us for Sunday tea. And there would be always a family friend or two.

The Herbert Place drawing-room, as I remember it, had a doubly watery character from being green in tone. On the light-green "trickle" (or *moiré*) wallpaper hung Florentine mirrors, not bright, wreathed in spiked gilt leaves. Between the mirrors hung sketches in gilt frames. The curtains were of green Morris tapestry, leaf-patterned. The chesterfield sofa and the armchairs were covered in pink-and-cream "shadow" cretonne. Lightness was given by frilled white muslin inner curtains, and the frilled white muslin slips (embroidered with harps and shamrocks) over the pink cushions on the sofas and chairs. The upright piano stood a little out from the wall. My mother's carved cherrywood writing-table was in the light of one of the two windows.

In this small town house, the drawing-room was the scene of my mother's personal life. Her books lay on the tables. (My father's study was on the ground floor, behind the dining-room.) Up on the first floor, overlooking the canal, my mother read, thought, and talked or wrote to her friends. On weekdays, to enter the drawing-room was to enter into intimacy with her. On Sundays, the room was more general, and more generally kind. After tea, the piano candles were lit, and before my going to bed we sang hymns around the piano. "Shall We Gather at the River?" was always the last, because it was my favourite hymn.

How shall I write "The End" to a book which is about the essence of a beginning? When I was seven years old, Herbert Place was given up: my father's mental illness had to be fought alone; my mother and I were ordered to England. The end of our Dublin house, in actual time, places no stop to my memories. Only a few of these have been written here. I have halted (not stopped) in the drawing-room, for it was there that, with my first comprehension of life as being other than mine, the second phase of my memories had its start.

Afterthoughts

PIECES ON WRITING

REFLECTIONS

THE ROVING EYE

How, AND WHY, does the writer find the subject—*his* subject—which germinates into play or story, poem or novel? Is this a matter of chance, or of expert calculation? The question, natural enough, is not easy to answer in natural terms—hence the growth around literary art of a myth or mystery. Writers are not secretive, but they are shy—shy behind the façade they learn to put up, and most shy about what is most simple to them. The fact is, they are of a childishness which could seem incredible, and which is more than half incredible to their thinking selves. The childishness is necessary, fundamental—it involves a perpetual, errant state of desire, wonder, and unexpected reflex. The writer, unlike his non-writing adult friend, has no predisposed outlook; he seldom observes deliberately. He sees what he did not intend to see; he remembers what does not seem wholly possible. Inattentive learner in the schoolroom of life, he keeps some faculty free to veer and wander. His is the roving eye.

By that roving eye is his subject found. The glance, at first only vaguely caught, goes on to concentrate, deepen; becomes the vision. Just what *has* he seen, and why should it mean so much? The one face standing forward out of the crowd, the figure in the distance crossing the street, the glare or shade significant on a building, the episode playing out at the next table, the image springing out of a phrase of talk, the disproportionate impact of some one line of poetry, the reverberation after a street accident or tiny subjective echo of a huge world event, the flare-up of visual memory or of sensuous memory for which can be traced no reason at all—why should this or that be of such importance as to bring all else to a momentous stop? Fate has worked, as in a falling in love—the writer, in fact, first knows he has found his subject by finding himself already obsessed by it. The outcome of obsession is, that he writes—rationalization begins with his search for language. He must (like the child who cannot keep silent) share, make known, communicate what he has seen, or knows. The urgency of what is real to him demands that it should be realized by other people.

It might, it appears, be said that writers do not find subjects: subjects find them. There is not so much a search as a state of open susceptibility. Can, and still more should, the state deliberately be maintained? At the outset it is involuntary, unconscious; when it is less so it loses some of its worth. "Relax, become blank, be passive"—should one advocate that? No, surely: nothing can happen to an inactive man; life shuns and experience forsakes him. Temperamentally, the writer exists on happenings, on contacts, conflicts, action and reaction, speed, pressure, tension. Were he a contemplative purely, he would not write. His moments of intake are inadvertent; not only that, but they may occur in what seems the very heart of the mêlée. How, then, and in what sense is he to pull out? How shall he keep unstaled his peculiar inner faculty for experience, his awareness of *the* experience, his susceptibility?

The essential is, that he be not imposed upon. He must know his own—that is, when it comes to subject. Truth is in his eye, in that roving eye: there are, and should never cease to be, unmistakable moments of recognition. Yet such moments may be daunting and inacceptable—"*Must* this be my subject?" the writer sighs. He is not so young perhaps; he foresees with dismay endless demands and challenges, a required break with all he knows of technique, a possible inadequacy of his powers, cold critics, a baffled public, a drop in sales. Can there be no alternative? There are, of course, a dozen: lively, factitious, tempting—the deflected writer writes with sinister ease: what he has lost, or that he is lost himself, he may if he is fortunate never know. But the true, abandoned subject takes its revenge.

The outward, apparent tie between writer and subject is not fortuitous. Background, origin, circumstance, the events of life, may be found to account, clearly enough, for a writer's trend and predispositions—his choice of scene, his pitch of mood, or his view of persons. A man's whole art may be rendered down, by analysis, to variations upon a single theme. A novelist's cast of characters may, from book to book, seem to be repetitions of one another. Or, regional colour lends a sort of rich, enchanted monotony to an entire output. Recurrence of images, the shape and blend of style, give to individual writing a sort of signature. But all that is not *subject:* subject remains apart—an inexplicable factor, an inner choice for which no external can yet account. The child, almost any child, is born with the hope that the universe is somehow to be explained: it may be the writer does not outlive that hope—here and there his eye passes, from clue to clue. Through subject, he offers his explanation. But can he say so—how be as simple as that?

It is for the critic, perhaps, to perceive, and say. Concentration on any one writer's work almost always ends by exposing a core of naïveté—a core which, once it has been laid bare, seems either infantile or august. There is little *inner* complexity, after all: the apparent outer complexity of the art has been little more than the effort towards expression. Somewhere within the pattern, somewhere behind the words, a responsive, querying innocence stays intact. There is, there must be, always the husk of thought. Intellectually, the writer ought to desire and must expect to confront in his critic one who is his intellectual match; it may be, his intellectual senior. Mind meets mind: style must stand up to hard analysis; structure at once reveals and defies its faults; method is there to sustain query; imagery is to be sifted through. All the same, there comes a point in the judgment process when intellect brings itself to a natural stop: the final value is rated by intuition. The vital test is, the sense of truth in the vision—its clearness, its spontaneity, its authority. In the case of the giant writer, there is no doubt; though there lingers an element of surprise —Balzac and Tolstoi, Faulkner and Mauriac, confound as well as command us by their discoveries. Unsuspected meaning in everything shines out; yet, we have the familiar resheathed in mystery. Nothing is negative; nothing is commonplace. For is it not that the roving eye, in its course, has been tracing for us the lineaments of a fresh reality? Something has been beheld for the first time.

—The New York Times Book Review

DISLOYALTIES

"Isn't disloyalty as much the writer's virtue," asks Graham Greene, "as loyalty is the soldier's?" Taken out of its context, the remark is startling: it has place in a triangular correspondence in which the contemporary artist's relation to society is discussed.* From the letters, whose range is fairly wide, emerge two main topics: attitude and morality. Graham Greene, expanding the sentence quoted, goes on to say: "Loyalty confines us to accepted opinions: loyalty forbids us to comprehend sympathetically our dissident fellows; but disloyalty encourages us to roam experimentally through any human mind; it gives to the novel the extra dimension of sympathy."

Few novelists, few understanding critics, would dispute this, upon a second thought. The public may hesitate for a while longer—do we not, it may be inquired, look to creative writers to be the guardians and spokesmen of human values? Do they propose to swerve, to betray, to default? On his side, the writer might and probably should agree that human values are his concern, and that in so far as to register and to voice these makes him their guardian, he is their guardian. But the point is, also, that for him they are neither abstractions nor standing points; he perceives them to be in their nature not fixed but shifting. He cannot but be aware of the endlessness of human variation and dissonance, the doublings and twistings of mankind under the grip of circumstance and the pressure of life. The novelist's subject is not society, not the individual as a social unit, but the individual as he himself is, behind the social mask. As such, his

* *Why Do I Write?* An Exchange of Views between Elizabeth Bowen, Graham Greene, and V. S. Pritchett. London: Percival Marshall; 1948.

peculiarities are infinite. If the novel is to continue vital, the "extra dimension of sympathy" must be found.

This, a writer's concept of writers' virtue, may seem to conflict with the concept held by the public mind. Never has loyalty, on the face of it, been ranked higher than it is today: it has come to be an essential of our survival—so much so that to fail in any adherence undermines, it is felt, some part of civilization. It should be noted that Graham Greene does not denounce adherences or attack their merit—is not the *soldier's* virtue loyalty? What he has pointed out is, the danger to the writer of anything which may exercise a restrictive and ultimately a blinding hold. His ideal is, to be at once disabused and susceptible, and forever mobile. This is not easily come at; for indeed the writer has in an even greater degree than his fellow-man the disposition to be attached—ideas, creeds, persons, and ways of life first magnetize, then begin to absorb him. By temperament he has a high potential of that extreme of loyalty, fanaticism. To break off any adherence involves dismay, pain, loneliness, and the sense of loss. It is not for him a matter of infidelity but of abstinence—one cannot be clear enough as to the distinction between the two. In turning away from resting-places, from lighted doorways, to pursue his course into darker country, he carries with him a burden of rejected alternatives and troubling regrets. Graham Greene is advocating the harder road.

Restrictive loyalties, with their danger, vary in their temptation to the writer according to his personal cast or temperament. The division of novelists into types or kinds is misleading; so many cannot be classed. No creative person is purely intellectual— one may, however, distinguish the intellectual novelist, building upon a framework of ideas, from the aesthetic-intuitive, working mainly on memories and impressions. In one case, the seat of integrity is the brain; in the other, feeling. For the former are involved constant speculation, cognizance of his own day, scrutiny of current science and thought, consideration of history, measurement of experience. For such a mind, the arrival at any position is important, and abandonment of it constitutes a crisis. Each time the writer disengages himself, convulsively, from a faith or theory, he spreads—and knows that he spreads—disarray in his readers' ranks: he has gainsaid the demand for stability. Does he not, then, it is asked, know his own mind? It is his own mind— and perhaps that only—with its demands and exactions and refusals to compromise, that he knows. He has once more imperilled good faith out of the need for truth—which forever shifts and changes its form in front of him. It is when he seems most to be trusted that he mistrusts himself—may not his apparent arrival at any standpoint mean no more than a slackening down of his faculties?

The accounted disloyalties of the thinking writer are at least overt, clear-cut, and definite: they manifest themselves in the public view and have taken place, where he himself is concerned, well over the water-mark of consciousness. Those of the intuitive writer are more subtle, gradual, and are moreover to him the more disturbing in that they may be evident only to himself. For in this case the sphere of the art is feeling. The artist of this kind is often the child of a background, the product of an intensive environment —racial, local, or social. What he creates takes character from his own strongly personal and often also inherited sense of life. His loyalties are involuntary and inborn—not, like the intellectual's, of his choice or seeking—and are the more powerful for that. Psychologically if not actually he is a regionalist, in his work relying not only for subject but for atmosphere, texture, colour, and flavour upon the particular enclave which has given him birth. In return for the inspiration he owes pieties; his ancestor-worship— however much this may seem to be diluted by irony —is fundamental. His sensibility, during the first of his working years, repays its sheltering by making impressive aesthetic growth. He has not yet touched the limits or felt the remoteness of his peculiar world.

This cannot continue: gradually the pulse of the art flags, and the writer knows it; or else, he notices in his work that other death-symptom, which is repetition. Now is the time to make the break, to strike out, to establish at any price the new vital outside communication. He has exhausted his native air—can his imagination learn to breathe another?

This crisis, simultaneously felt in his personal being (because of debts and affections) and his aesthetic being, is the crux of the feeling writer's career. He cannot free himself from the hereditary influences without the sense of outraging, injuring, and betraying them—virtually, it appears to him, he must cease to honour his father and his mother. From the moment he has perceived this, there is no choice—the matter decides itself according to whether he is or is not a valid writer. To the outside world, the effect and outcome of the struggle is not at once apparent —all that may be observed is a hardening or harshening of the manner, or an unexpected tension between the writer and his accustomed subject—for he has not necessarily forsaken the old scenes; what has happened is that he sees them newly. Only the rare reader or the perceptive critic is able to detect the transition book.

The disloyalties of the writer, evidently, are not a privilege; they are a test and a tax. They are the inverse of an ultimate loyalty—to the pursuit, the search, the range of the exploration, the hope of the "extra dimension," wherein lies truth.

—*The New York Times Book Review*

AUTOBIOGRAPHY

AUTOBIOGRAPHY nowadays finds a public; perceptibly it is moving into the forefront of the literary scene. Old, in fact primitive, as a form of expression, it has been rediscovered—it is being more written and more read than it was, say, thirty years ago. How is this revived taste or addiction to be accounted for? What peculiar attraction has the self-told story, what arresting notes does it strike? Is it that the scales are tipping in favour of truth as against fiction, of the actual as against the invented? If so, is the rise of the autobiographer to be seen by the novelist as a danger signal, as a warning that his creative-inventive faculties are beginning to thin, falter, or run down, or that he is losing the formula for the illusion by whose strength fiction maintains its hold? "Everything," Flaubert said of his art, "is in the manner of the telling." To which he added elsewhere: "One must *interest.*" Herein may lie the clue: not that the novelist writes less well today, but that the autobiographer of today writes better.

At a glance the narration of one's own story might seem a simple matter, less a task than an outlet. The material is there ready to hand; the ego is flattered; the pen is willing. Indeed, for generations many excellent persons not only embarked upon but concluded their autobiographies without effort or qualm; all the undertaking required, as they saw it, was sufficient time, industry, self-confidence, and a reliable memory. Out into circulation, therefore, proceeded records of blameless, not uneventful, seldom quite unimportant lives. Rare was the author-protagonist who had not at least some reason to congratulate himself or who was altogether obscure—rank, celebrity, or honourable achievement as a rule warranted publication and guaranteed notice for the book. Here and there the aim was more limited: private printing for the benefit of family and friends. Most of those works have long ago been pulped and forgotten; some, whether by chance or piety, survive—in the dusky libraries of old houses or exposed on outside tables of the secondhand store. They are good for a laugh, but they merit a second thought.

Each has been someone's testament; pompous, stilted, naïve, shapeless, verbose, or unconsciously exhibitionistic they may be, but some continuous energy sustained them. One may find in turning over their pages some traces of a sterling belief in life, some unexpected attitude to society, some unresolved, therefore revealing, doubt, some uncalculated flicker of personality, or (which is most usual) the conviction that the writer's discoveries cast light, that his findings add to the sum of knowledge, and that his experience, often hard-won, cannot but be of use to his fellow-man. These bulky volumes, of which the Victorian age saw the full flush, are they not monuments to a vanished state, curiosities, likely sidelights on history, instances of our own mortal wish to preserve by any means from oblivion what has been valuable or dear? Literature, however, they are not.

It is as literature, not as the private document, that modern autobiography makes its claim. It is the product not of licensed ease but of a disciplined concentration—in fact, no longer an amateur affair.

The author seeks expression, as in any other art, but *self*-expression only at one remove—so much so that he may tend to be more detached, less impassioned than if he were writing the life of another man. This may go so far that in places he shows his tie with himself only by an omniscience as to his own affairs which would be impossible for an outside person. He attempts to place not only his background but also the scenes, faces, and events which are the constituents of his story at such a distance as to be in perspective. At the same time this quasi-outward view must alternate with a fearlessly inward one: he must flinch from no interior knowledge. The non-egocentric autobiography would be devoid of virtue, point, motive, meaning, or *raison d'être*. The "I" in the narrative stands for something more than consistent viewpoint or continuity; it provides the visionary element, in whose light all things told appear momentous and fresh—though they may not be new, though they may have happened before.

First and last it must be the writer's temperament which conditions the climate of the self-told story, his sense of proportion which sets its scale, his predilections, fancies, or curiosities which establish its psychological hinterland—what has it meant to me, so far, to be myself; in what so far has my being me involved me; how have I acted, reacted, impacted on other people in consequence? Such throughout seem to be the questions posed.

One might say that whereas autobiography used to

be based on statement, now it derives from query, being tentative rather than positive, no longer didactic but open-minded. It is mobile, exploratory. This may come from the fact that today it is less often written in old age; it is, rather, the work of early or late maturity. Is it not at this point, about halfway through the journey, that we do all have an instinct to pause, look back, and reflect? The autobiographer's impulse has synchronized with that of his fellow-man; he is speaking not only to but for his contemporaries. That mood which engenders autobiography is known to many who do not take up the pen.

Few of us lack as we grow older an objective regard for our own lives—for the distance covered in sheer time, whether or not in space, and for the individual tracks we have left behind us. We have not merely survived, we have continued to *be,* and, which is still more, to be aware of being. Existence (unless one is so unhappy as to lose or be deprived of one's taste for it) becomes more rather than less interesting as it progresses; gradually one's years in the world add up to something which takes on size and shape and in which meaning may at least be sought for. The least exceptional of us possesses his own experience, unique if only in being uniquely his—apparently, he may have conformed since birth and may expect to conform till death to the mass-pattern, but there have been moments along the way of which only he knows the spring or core. Few lives, however seemingly trivial, conventional, flat, or tame, have not held some unguessed-at secret, some inner story; there has been the ordeal of some decision, the realization of some desire, or the abandonment of some hope. An internal drama may have resolved itself; a drama still unnoticed may have come to its crux. And outside all this has stood, like a mask or frame, the man's external doings among his fellows—at work, in society, at home. To these, too, interest attaches as he looks back: gains and losses, changes and chances, trials and errors, make a tale of their own. Above all, to study the contrast, the interplay between the inner and outer "I," may be fascinating—how much so only oneself can know.

"Yes," decides the average person, "if I were to write my life, it would make quite a book. Suppose I did, who would read it? Why—I suppose nobody." In ninety-nine cases out of a hundred he would be right. A man's own life has for himself more interest, significance, and importance than he can hope to convey to the rest of the world. Good sense warns most of us that we would not be competent to do anything like justice to our own stories. What, then, is the secret of the autobiographer who by writing both entertains and satisfies thousands of readers unknown to him? Is it merely that he "knows how to write"? There is more than that: he has forged an art of his own—he succeeds, in fact, in a task which, while it might seem humanly straightforward, is fraught with aesthetic problems, difficulties, and tests.

To begin with he must pinpoint his own identity;

yet at the same time show within himself the accepted workings of human nature. There may be more than a touch of the unusual, even of the extraordinary, about what he has thought or felt or what has happened to him; but the ordinary has to be kept in mind. As a rule, by the time he sits down to write he has already made his name by achievement: it is for him to suggest the value (to himself) and still more the place in his life of what he has made or done. What at the start had been his ruling ambition? How far has this been realized—in his view? It is unlikely (given the present-day age for writing) that he regards his career as closed—therefore what next? Are there mistakes or omissions he intends to repair before again moving forward; or is he headed impatiently toward new ground?

Autobiography is, above all, narrative; like any other story, it ought not to be clogged by too much analysis. Hence one more advantage of its being written in middle life—neither youth's trend towards introspection nor old age's urge to post-mortem is to be feared. At the same time there must be an element of the self-portrait—and of a self-portrait, moreover, executed in public, touch by touch. Do we not discover the man as he discovers himself; even at times may our knowledge of him seem to run a little ahead of his? It is part of the autobiographer's courteous guile, his art, to allow us revelations he does not seem to share. Be certain, he knows what he is doing.

Granted, his material is to hand: not for him are

the labours of invention. But the sheer mass, the variety of that material, might create a predicament of its own—what should he leave out, what is he to put in? Fortunately, he does not, cannot, remember everything: would it be obvious to say that he puts in what he recalls most clearly? And rightly; memory is selective, and adamant as to its selections—arbitrary, tricky, patchy though these may appear to be. The boldly left gaps, the admitted lacunae in the narrative of the modern autobiographer are themselves telling; moreover, they guarantee the veracity of what has been written down. Next after choice comes the question of order; it may be noted how often events are reft from their sequence (in time: that is) to be grouped with others with which they link or compare—used, in fact, to enhance each other's significance. And that pictorialness, the visual magic by which landscapes, cities, faces, gardens, rooms, dresses, are conjured back into sight—is that mere decoration? Surely not. "I am a part of all that I have seen." Out of impressions, no less than thought and feeling, is the texture of an existence spun. To ignore sensation would be to fail in telling the whole, which is the true, story.

Most of all are we not commanded by that hint of an even slowly emerging pattern? Autobiography as we know it now is artists' work; though pegged to one man's story it has as its subject Life, as by one man that has been found to be. The findings may not be ours; the subject is. What would be your, my finding?—your, my pattern? One man addresses the potential autobiographer in us all.

—Saturday Review of Literature

SOURCES OF INFLUENCE

IN STUDYING the development of an artist, the factor of influences upon him must, I imagine, always be taken into account. Analysis of influence, its general force and its particular workings, devolves in the main on the critic and art-historian: this field is held to require specialized knowledge and aesthetic discernment possessed by few. By the rest of us, painting, sculpture, music, architecture, may be enjoyed without being historically comprehended: we react, that is to say, to the masterpiece without thought as to what may have been its complex origin. Where it is a matter of colour, form used plastically, or pure sound, we are inclined to leave the genesis of the work of art to the trained mind. But where the medium is language, all is different—words are the general property; they link with *our* experience, so the creative use of them comes within our critical scope. The writer is less at a distance than other artists; one does not require to be a specialist to study him. His evolution, the processes of his formation, lie open to any reader who cares enough—in this case, where influence is at work it almost always can be suspected, if not detected. The writer is amongst us; in number writers multiply every day; in our epoch writing, of all the arts, evokes most social interest and most human concern. With regard, then, to writers let us consider influence.

One may classify influences, one may trace them, one may discuss whether, in a particular instance, such-and-such an influence has acted favourably. What one cannot do, with any profit, is, attempt to answer that frequent question—whether it is a "good" thing to be influenced, or not. Influence, in one sense if not another, is inevitable. The question as to whether it should or should not be avoided therefore falls to the ground—yet does (not only because it is asked often but because it is asked seriously) deserve respect. The idea of "good," in this context, probably has an ethical no less than aesthetic background— there is a latent notion that the writer subjecting himself to influence (from, presumably, another literary source) is in some way practising a dishonesty, advancing through using a borrowed power, or endangering what should be most sacred, in being most original, in his own talent. This objection to influence may be due to confusion—that is, failure to distinguish—between influence and out-and-out imitation: the latter *is* a malpractice; it is also calculated and voluntary. It might, indeed, not be too much to say that the distinction between influence and imitation demarcates, equally, the imaginatively creative from the merely cerebrally inventive writer. Where writing is a matter of invention, and nothing more, there may well be a temptation to copy the successful inventions of other people. Imagination, though by its nature susceptible and affectable, tends all the time to the *new*; it is bored by the secondhand.

Susceptibility, it should be understood, plays a great part in the make-up of the creative writer. He is susceptible to environment, to experience, and, in the same way and not less, to styles and energies in already existing art. From all three sources he is attracting influences; all of which will leave their mark on his work. It is the third, the aesthetic-literary, which is most easily recognized by the reader; and for which the writer is most often called to account, and indeed reproached. Style—the actual choice and rhythm of words—most often carries an influence, and most clearly shows it. But with style, vision and outlook are interknit: did not Flaubert call style "a manner of seeing"? As we all know, a strongly directed film or a striking collection of pictures by one artist can so invade the receptive eye that, coming out of the cinema or the gallery, one continues for hours after to see life in terms of So-and-so's film or So-and-so's painting. A creative manner of seeing is infectious—small wonder that writers at the tentative stage find it hard to shake off the magic effect of a master's vision. And this may be true not only of visual but of moral angle. In fiction one senses the power, these days, of affective novelists such as Henry James, Faulkner, and Mauriac (unalike to each other as these may be).

The literary influence on a writer is, of all three, likely to be the most transient, ending with the period of apprenticeship—indeed, being a form of apprenticeship in itself. Throughout his oscillations from style to style, his experiments in manner after manner, the writer is making his own growth. He will shell off, one by one—he may even react against—the influences which have up to a point fostered his growth. At the same time, he will have absorbed something; and he will continue to owe something to his place as a link in art's continuity. As he reaches maturity, and himself tends to become an influence, he in his turn will be transmitting something—there is an honourable, nay, necessary artistic heredity. As to literary influence, we may leave it that only uncertain talent stifles during this phase: the stamp of inherent originality is that sooner or later, and sooner rather than later, it must emerge.

The influence of environment is the most lasting; and except in the case of "regional" writers, operates deepest down. Sometimes, the force of environment may be felt by a writer's conscious, sharp reaction against it. Admittedly, it is the atmosphere of the scenes of youth which is most often decisive—though it has happened that, some way on into life, a writer has stumbled upon a place, perhaps an entire country, which he in some way recognizes, which seems to claim him, and which offers a hitherto lacking inspiration to his art. In that case, there is a sort of psychological adoption: a new phase of freshness of feeling, equivalent to a second childhood, sets in. But the majority are haunted by the shadowy, half-remembered landscape of early days: impressions and feelings formed there and then underlie language, dictate choices of imagery. In writing, what is poetically spontaneous, what is most inimitably individual, has this source—the writer carries about in him an inner environment which is constant; though which also, as time goes on, tends to become more and more subjective.

One must remember that the inner environment has been always, to a degree, selected: as we now know, there is an element of choice, however apparently involuntary, in memory. The writer is influenced by what he retains; and still more, perhaps, by the very fact that he has retained it—and the picture, by continuous dwelling upon, may be so much intensified as to become changed. Thus, though to an extent the environment creates the writer, he also plays a part in creating it—his art, by demanding this kind of sustenance, has reached back past the bounds of actual memory into a phantasmagoric hinterland quite its own.

Experience as an influence needs least comment: this is taken for granted—perhaps too much so. There is a tendency to think that the direct transcription of experience (into novel or poem) and the *action* of experience are synonymous. True action of experience on the creative powers is erratic, indirect, and slow—also, in so far as writers do make use of their individual experience as persons, they almost invariably transform it. The experience which really influences art does not consist in drama or incidents; it is a sort of emotional accumulation, or, at its best, a slowly acquired deep-down knowledge. Experience is the reaction to what happens, not the happening itself—and in that sense experience is, like environment, to a degree selected. The meaning which is extracted from occurrences varies, and varies in its importance, according to the writer's choice as to feeling: he allows some things to "take" with him more than others. The catastrophic disaster, the sudden primitive joy, are of course irresistible: they improve themselves. These leave behind in the writer what he has most in common with humanity: it is by its power to co-ordinate what is major with what is small in life that the soundness of his art is to be tested.

Is it true that the writers of our day are too much subject to influence, from whatever source? Do they lack the resilience, the independent hardiness of their predecessors? Literary influence (the first) seems harder now to throw off than once it was: it has been said that we have too many disciples, too few masters. If this be so, it may be found that, as a generation, we writers are in a transitional, learning stage: the task of expression appears a vast one—the old simplicities of the world are gone; the artist is hard-pressed by what is happening round him. Our century, as it takes its frantic course, seems barely habitable by humans: we have to learn to survive while we learn to write. And *to* write, we must draw on every resource; to express, we need a widened vocabulary—not only as to words, as to ideas. The apprentice stage, given modern necessities, cannot be a long one: some of us there may be who will not outlive it. But at least we are keeping going a continuity: we may serve to link the past with the future masters.

—*Saturday Review of Literature*

EXCLUSION

THOUGH one may speak of a novel in terms of its length or shortness, one has in mind something more —its effective size. The book's physical bulk, its number of pages, by no means denote, or act as a measure for, the extent or depth of its hold on imagination. The content of the novel is what affects us; and the content, because it expands in the reader's mind, may by far exceed what is stated in the actual writing—this, in fact, is one evidence of creative power. In some few cases, the giving of this expansive force may be a fluke of the author's genius, but more often it is considered aim; and—genius admittedly being rare—it is with the aim that we are concerned. Experience, innate sense of his craft, and a critical estimate of the work of others combine to teach the author that what may be most eloquent, sometimes, is the excluded word—or phrase, or paragraph, or it may be chapter. He learns that elimination may serve expression. He comes to see how far the unstated builds up the content.

82

For the author's purpose is not merely to tell much, it is to make known the whole—the whole being his concept, which is his novel. The making known, and its manner, is what concerns him. What kind of telling, and how much, can and should best go to the making known? Continuously the author must be deciding not only how but exactly *what* to tell. He will be seeking, somewhere within himself, the reasons for the statements he is to make and, not less, the reasons for his withholdings. That the withheld (from actual writing) is not necessarily the rejected cannot be made too clear: indeed, what is withheld plays a creative part—the author, by keeping some things back, is adding silent potentials to his story. He makes felt, in fact, what he feels but has never said. He says (or, rather, writes and allows to stand) only what does gain, from his point of view, by being told in so many words. The gain is definite ground in the reader's memory—a base, perhaps, to take off from later on. There must *be* factual groundwork: statement takes care of fact. There is much that the reader relies upon being told; therefore much of writing is bound to be informative—as to what is happening, to whom, and where, and when. So much is the bone-structure of story-telling. Novel-writing, however, is more than that: it is when we come to the narrative's "why's" and "how's," the complex causes of action, the ripples of its effect, the shadowy ambience of the personality, that we touch what makes the essential *novel*. We pass outside the ranges of concrete fact:

more will be needed, from now on, than direct telling. Perception, evaluation, are called to come into play. From now on, the writer must cause the reader to perceive and evaluate for himself—or, at least, to imagine that he does so.

In so far as the writer has known more than he says, the reader will in his turn draw from the pages more than is there in print. More will appear to him to exist, more will appear to him to be going on than has been described or recounted. One assumes, of course, that the reader brings to the novel a certain capacity of his own—that he has not only knowledge but sense of life, ready to be stimulated further. He will have faculties ready to respond, a power of judgment gleaned from his own experience, and a wish that experience, as he already knows it, may perhaps yet yield up some more meaning. The reader, if he be of such a kind, will be predisposed to react to the novel fully (that is, if the novel has lifelike fullness) and with perhaps more intensity than he would to life. He cannot, however, add to the novel what is not already there—there, that is, in being known by the author, though not necessarily in words set down. For this reason, the whole of the novel *as* a whole—every possible aspect of the characters (not merely aspects relevant to the plot) and every possibility, implication, angle, or incident of the plot (apart from the parts played by the characters)—ought to be an imaginative reality for the author, conceived absolutely, existing completely, circumstantial down to

84

the last detail. Where the author has failed to know, there will be a vacuum, which cannot but be come upon by the reader. The writer's failure to realize, at any point, may flaw the reality of the whole.

Here are instances of the demand for knowledge: It may sound a commonplace to say that the author should know his characters: do we grasp, though, what such knowingness comprehends? First, outwardly, all must be known *about* them—race, class, heredity, place and date of birth, the environment of the youth and childhood, education, profession, amount of income or salary, family life (if any), place and nature of residence, and career or adventures up to the point where the character enters our given story. In fact, as to each of his men and women the author does well to compile a dossier, written or otherwise—if not written, kept ready in the file of the mind. Why? Because outer circumstance, in itself important, does also work on the inner being. And when it does come to the inner beings, the author must, in each of his cases, know those with a sort of passionless depth. His penetrating closeness to his characters can have the virtue (rarer with intimacies in real life) of being almost unclouded by emotion. And, in one way, he has the possibility of knowing them better than he knows himself; for he is unlikely to have the time, the occasion, or the inclination to watch himself either as continuously or with the same fervour as he watches them. It may of course be said that he is creating his characters *by* knowing them:

in the early stage of his relations with them that may be true; but later they gain objective reality, turn round and begin to teach him about themselves. Complete and detached as beings, they reveal, as beings do, complexities, inconsistencies, contradictions; and, through being three-dimensional, they take on shadow. From then on, the author (who has become their chronicler, and nothing more) can do no more than apprehend them, guess at them. At the same time their conduct, the way they both act and are, begins to show variations and alternatives. . . . Feeling that, the author must convey his sense of that to his reader. If he fails to feel that, his characters remain for the reader unrealized, "thin." At the same time, the reader demands that, for the plot, the characters should be so simplified as to be comprehensible.

For the plot, as related (or told) by the author to reader, an apparent simplicity is essential. And yet, what is told to have happened must gain significance, background, from what is not told. The story's action, for instance, may take place on a Friday; but the reader must sense, through the author's knowing, what sort of Wednesday, Thursday, led up to it, and what sort of Saturday, Sunday, are to follow. Also the alternatives to the plot, owing to the latent alternatives in the behaviour of the characters, must be felt by the reader up to the last moment—it is indeed in this that suspense consists; and no novel, whether the action in it be psychological or physical, ought to omit the factor of suspense. The existence, inside the author's mind, of a possible, far vaster range of the plot than is ever told gives what *is* told, for the reader, certainty and validity. . . . The same is true with regard to the scenes of happenings, which must be by the author envisaged down to the final detail, though descriptions of them must not be categoric.

In short, the "must's" and "must not's" of effectual novel-writing entail embarkation, by the author, upon something far wider, deeper, and longer than what, in print, *in statement,* he will eventually present. He will accumulate, in the course of his work, a mass of what is to him reality, with all the time the knowledge that much of it must remain, ultimately, extraneous. Extraneous to what? His aesthetic purpose. His eventual book is, he intends, to be wieldy, shapely, and unencumbered: if statements are to make their expected point, he dare not clog the imagination of the reader with too much of them, or distract the mind of the reader by too many. As to the solution, nothing offers a rule but trained instinct or the immediate finding. The test of what *is* to be said, told, written (or, to remain in writing), is its connection with what has been said before, its relevance to the aesthetic purpose, and, not least, its power to make known, by suggestion or evocation of something further, what needs to be known without being told. From the unsaid, or from what does not remain in writing, comes a great part of the potency of the novel.

One speaks of what does, or does not, remain in

writing, because of many authors who put work into pages they later destroy, or who complete scenes only to throw them out. I myself do so. I see that the sense or trend of what has been written almost always survives: it is there by inference—and further, expressive action which has been "cut" still somehow makes its effect, from off-stage. Other authors frame scenes or conceive of actions in their own minds only, yet with a thoroughness which, till they *are* abandoned, gives them the status of written work—and here, too, nothing goes quite for nothing. Master novelists, Tolstoi, Balzac, give the impression of having held nothing back; their books' length tallies with their effective size. And less splendidly, that is so with Trollope and Thackeray. We, today, query whether actual writing can any longer carry the full charge: we have the art, the policy of exclusion. In their aim for size, our novels are partly silence: we seek what tells. By our own means, we seek to keep for the novel the veracity, the authority of the work of art.

ADVICE

"I WRITE with enjoyment, fluently, freely, yet my finished work discourages me—it lacks something. Should I not form a style—and if so, how?"

"My writing, I feel, is too self-conscious: I am inhibited by the idea of style. Should I not perhaps throw style overboard and aim for absolute spontaneity?"

Those are two honest questions, both asked often. While they represent opposite points of view, both touch the core of a writer's intrinsic problem—the method and manner of expression. We may assume that the speaker, in either case, feels the urge of what he or she has to say: what comes next is, How can this best be said? How, on the one hand, can strength, shape, finish, and a degree of beauty be given to what seems rough or inchoate work? And on the other, how can the writer avoid sacrificing naturalness? There is an equal danger in obsession with style and in disregard for it, and a not less, a perhaps more prevalent, danger in misconceiving what style is. There has come to be something abstract about the word—so much so, I think, that we may do well to leave *style* for the moment aside and speak of *language*, with something of what that comprehends.

Language is the writer's medium, used by him as the painter uses form, line, and colour. The attribute of language should be livingness—that is, not a word should be so employed as to give out a dull or deadening ring or seem to have exhausted its significance. About the choice, in each given context, of noun, verb, adverb, or adjective there is really something momentous, vital; for each of these is a statement, each is a small reality which is, again, to serve to build up the composite reality of the whole—be that poem, novel, or story. "How am I to know," the

89

sometimes despairing writer asks, "which the right word is?" The reply must be: "Only *you* can know. The right word is, simply, the wanted one; the wanted word is the one most nearly true. True to what? Your vision and your purpose." Sometimes it may happen that such a word springs immediately, happily to the mind—some thoughts, it seems, are born ready-clad in language—at other times it must be most patiently sought for. As to the variation in the difficulty one has with words, let us discuss that a little later; now we must halt at a certain warning as to that ease with which they, also, can come.

For there is no doubt that just as we have addictions in other matters—colours, scents, kinds of person—we are subject to the same in regard to words. Some are pleasurable, attractive, fascinating to us; others seem negative or distasteful. Taste as to language, like taste as to other things, may have roots for which only the analyst can account; or, again, it may stem from associations that can be frankly traced, or from discipleship to some older writer who gives certain words prestige by effective use. For whatever cause, it may happen, at any age, that our favourites come to dominate our vocabulary, and may even influence our thought. We do therefore have to be on the watch—not necessarily against the word that springs to the mind at once, but against the word that springs to the mind too temptingly, too easily, and *too often*. Habitual turns of phrase, habitual words, are literary counterparts of besetting sins—and they are certainly the enemies of expression: they restrict or wither the freshness of our way of seeing. And the same is true of those binding prose-rhythms into which (maybe in the pursuit of "style") some writers tend to let themselves fall. Repetitive sentence-shapes and paragraph-patterns make for something worse than monotony: they become conventions. And conventions in writing are no less deadening for being conventions of one's own—it is perhaps these which are most insidious.

Our language must on no account be allowed to set or harden; all the time we must let it extend its range, keep it on the move, have it remain open—open, that is to say, to a constant, refreshing intake of the new. Not because there is virtue in sheer novelty, but because a word not known or employed before brings with it the further volume of its own meaning with which to amplify our expressive power. It is grievous to have to leave unsaid something we wished to say because it does not seem to us that the thing can *be* said: it is sad to leave what we feel only half-conveyed. Clearly we are obstructed by lack of words: that apparent lack may be simply want of the sense of the implication and content words can have—even familiar words may yield up what we did not once foresee. To widen and deepen vocabulary, to command it, we need not necessarily take up what might be called a collector's attitude to the dictionary: excellent though it is to acquire new nouns, verbs, adverbs, and adjectives, it is better still to explore those we have and know. Language is a mixture of statement and evocation: the test of its livingness, for a writer, is the extent of its power to conjure up. When we write we endeavour to be exact, but also we must be sensitive, imaginative as to words themselves —for they are there not merely to serve *our* purpose: they are charged with destinies of their own, haunted by diverse associations.

Novelty in expression is by no means to be sought for its own sake: it may become a danger if too obtrusive. In general, showy, striking, aggressive words are to be avoided—they throw writing out of pitch: they distract the reader. Though words to the writer are of intense concern, it should be his object to make the reader as little aware of them as possible.

We wish to implant in the reader's mind identically what we have in our own; we wish him to see as clearly and feel as sharply as we do with regard to our subject. We are creating for him something, new to ourselves, that for him, too, has never been there before. We shall, however, only defeat our purpose if we expose the mechanics by which the thing is done. Our ideal therefore, must be a language as clear as glass—the person looking out of the window knows there *is* glass there, but he is not concerned with it; what concerns him is what comes through from the other side. When we, as writers, are reading what we admire of other creative work, we often find we react, subtly and strongly, with a blend of aesthetic and human pleasure, to something from a particular line or page. Only then (and then only, perhaps, because we *are* writers) do we look back, marvelling, trying to analyze how this was brought about. And how often that line, sentence, or page proves striking only by its utter simplicity—how much art has gone toward that simplicity we are not to know.

This agreed, there is something not to forget. There is a dramatic element in language, which is latent even while held in check. And there are, we must recognize, situations in writing when the check may be fearlessly removed. For the poet this occurs often—in fact, it is probable that for him the check need hardly come into play at all: the poet, as compared to the prose writer, is like someone driving a more highly powered car at greater speed for a shorter distance. He needs high tension rather than staying power, but for the short-storyist and the novelist, all-out release of language must only come infrequently and, when it does, advisedly. Climax of drama in the story justifies fullness of drama in the language. Then is the time for arresting words—we may resort to vocabulary as a striking power. The discordant, the odd, the harsh, the cacophonous, all assault, by shock tactics, the amazed but no less receptive reader. Need we stress that obvious shock tactics miss their mark? "Strong" or purple passages, indecencies, the florid or hysterical piling up of adjectives, italics, exclamation marks, rows of dots, and so on are likely merely to bore or numb, or to arouse resistance in a derisive form. What *is* effective is the

affray of words, the vibrating force of their unfore-
seenness, their clash upon or contrast with one another. Why do we react more to "the thin gate
clanged" than to "the iron gate shut noisily"?

Language can not only register but heighten, by its
speed, its emphasis, and its rhythm, the emotional
pressure we put behind it. Not only the literary but
the psychic difference between the long and the short
sentence is very marked: and we should make the
most of the variation. There should be variation, too,
in what we may call the texture of our prose—that is,
some passages are the better for being written lightly;
others demand a packed, possibly somewhat "difficult" concentration of ideas and images. The former
passages, probably, will be either narrative or dialogue; the latter, analysis or description. Always try to
simplify, is the rule—but there remain complexities
which must be battled through. The imperative, in
fact the essential, thing, is that variations in writing,
from page to page, should correspond with what is
going on concurrently in the writer's mood *and* in the
actual story. Proust saw writing as a form of transla-
tion: we do, by the process of finding and fitting
words, attempt to capture a thousand otherwise fleeting sensations, feelings, impressions, lights and
shadows, and half-thoughts. Language must be a
strong though fine net.

And so, what of style—and our two beginning
questions? I have, in speaking rather of language,

hoped to break down that other, too abstract concept. For each writer there can be only one style—his own; the problem in each case is how to arrive at it. Style is a matter of coming to terms with language. Need I explain that by this I mean natural terms? You have one thing to say, I another: by both of us, and for both of us, the most nearly ideal manner has to be found. Your language could not be mine, nor mine yours; for our subjects differ, and every subject demands, by its unique nature, a unique kind of expression. In our individual workings we have the same aims—clearness, truth, evocation, some touch of grace. By keeping those in view, we arrive at style —it may be almost imperceptibly. Only to see style wrongly makes us cramped or "conscious." Style is not a mere surface to be adorned from without: the spring of it is deep-down, interior. It stays mobile, and stays alive, through its organic relation to its subject. Are then style and language identical? Not quite: one might call style the effect of language. And by slowly mastering language we reach the right, the no-other, expression of what there is to say.

—Mademoiselle

PREFACES

DOCTOR THORNE *

I

"Doctor Thorne," says Anthony Trollope in his *Auto-biography,* "has, I believe, been the most successful book I have ever written." His immense production gives the remark force. The success of this particular novel still surprised him when, near the end, he looked back on his working life—does it surprise us, after a hundred years? There are lasting characteristics; before we count them let us look at the book in its own day. *Doctor Thorne* was first published, in

* *Doctor Thorne,* by Anthony Trollope. Boston: Riverside Editions, Houghton Mifflin Company; 1959.

London, in 1858. Third of the "Chronicles of Barset," it was at the advantage of being set in a landscape already known, and of reintroducing (if by reference, chiefly) characters to whom amusement or liking already attached. At the same time, while it consolidated the ground won by its Barset predecessors (*The Warden, Barchester Towers*), *Doctor Thorne* was in no limiting sense their sequel—if it gained by the carry-over of former interest, this third tale lost no time in creating its own. The main cast had the attraction of being new-comers; one could start from scratch in the matter of curiosity. Also, excellent as had been, twice over, the Barchester entertainment, the cathedral's shadow and the close's confines could have set up a species of claustrophobia —now, one moved out into the open country: *Doctor Thorne* was rural in an English way, as England loves best to be. Nor were streets and spires all that one left behind. The two former plots had turned upon power politics, with the romantic element little more than subsidiary. Here came a love story pure and simple—or so far so as a love story can be.

Trollope wrote this novel in the ideal mood, at what was for him the ideal time. He did not, as it happened, think of the plot himself: visiting his mother and brother in Italy, he was faced by something of a dilemma. "I had finished *The Three Clerks* just before leaving England, and when in Florence was cudgelling my brain for a new plot. Being with my brother, I asked him to sketch me a plot, and he drew out that of my next novel, called *Doctor Thorne*. I mention this particularly," continues the honest man, "because it was the only occasion in which I have had recourse to some source other than my own brain for the thread of a story." The aid was timely; the Trollope brother was clever—not so much in devising the plot (which in parts is cumbrous), but in seeing it to be the outlet for Anthony. Or this may have been a happy fortuity. Either way, it was the *idea* for the coming novel, rather than the provided "thread," which mattered—the idea ignited material Trollope had in him, and had not so far used; further, it served to unlock powers, and allowed for the exercise of addictions, of whose pressure he may not have been aware. He had come to a point in his development at which *Doctor Thorne* was the novel for him to write.

Far from ideal were the conditions under which the story was set on paper. A great part of *Doctor Thorne* was written at sea, during a terribly rough voyage from Marseilles to Alexandria. "I wrote my allotted number of pages every day. On this occasion more than once I left my paper on the cabin table, rushing away to be sick in the privacy of my state room. . . . *Labor omnia vincit improbus*. I do not say that to all men has been given physical strength sufficient for such exertion as this, but I do believe that real exertion will enable most men to work at almost any season." Never can thoughts of calm inland landscape have been sweeter than then, on the heaving Mediterranean. Barsetshire's acres, Greshamsbury's village street, the great house lawns, and the doctor's parlour could have endeared themselves simply as *terra firma*. Alternating between the throes of seasickness, were they beheld with especial ardour? At many times, as his talent went on to ripen, Trollope had this power of fixing vision: scenes he depicts have, often, glow and rotundity—one must not attribute too much to that February voyage. If there was not one reason for idealization, there was another; underlyingly there was a temperamental one.

The reception of his first books had been disappointing; there was something, however, in his having written them at all. The environment and happenings of his youth had militated against any kind of confidence. Born in 1815, Anthony came to consciousness as the son of a failed barrister, a poor gentleman—a man of savage integrity of intellect, hopeless incompetence in business, irritable temper, and fatal pride. Everything the father touched went to ruin; successive attempts at farming, on land near London, sank the family into outright poverty—throughout which the unfortunate Mr. Trollope was dominated, always, by his obsession: his sons must be educated as gentlemen. The boys were to follow in his footsteps, going first to great English schools, later to Oxford. The children were six in number: only two, Anthony and a brother, had the stamina to live on into maturity. Mrs. Trollope, in whom calmness of temper was matched by courage and, it was to prove, ability, struggled to prop up the family fortunes. First, she took ship to America, where she opened a bazaar in Cincinnati: "Money might be made by sending goods —little goods such as pin-cushions, pepper-boxes and pocket-knives—out to the still unfurnished States." The enterprise failed, but not before the quick-witted lady had garnered in material for a hurriedly written book, *The Domestic Manners of the Americans*. The success (in England) of this, and the name it made for her, embarked Mrs. Frances Trollope on authorship; thereafter, money came in, if never so fast as it ran out. She wrote, wrote; she could not afford to stop. Anthony watched her at work between two sickrooms, a dying husband's, a dying son's. This heroine's story deserved telling; here, we consider her effect on our author. If her example inspired him later on, her industry, and his dependence on it, added reproach to the gloom of the early years. "Now and then there would arise a feeling that it was hard upon my mother that she should have to do so much for us, that we should be idle while she was forced to work so constantly . . ."

But the worst wounds to confidence, and those slowest in healing, were dealt elsewhere. Anthony, as the *Autobiography* wryly tells us, enjoyed the distinction of being miserable at two of England's most famous schools: Harrow and Winchester. His fellow-pupils came sometimes from noble, always from reputable families; if not from the aristocracy, from the landed gentry or upper ranks of the professional classes. They had mellow backgrounds, promising futures—unhappily, by the showing of the *Autobiography,* their characters did not justify their good fortune. Forced, at a disadvantage, into this gilded company, the insecure shabby lad paid the full price for his father's fanaticism. To Harrow, not far from his home, he went as a day boy—a status considerably despised. At Winchester (where his father had been before him) he was received at greatly reduced fees: this was common knowledge, and it was known no less when what *was* owing ceased to be paid. Removed from Winchester under a cloud of shame, he returned with ignominy to Harrow—walking twelve miles daily to and fro through the lanes for a schooling from which, it appears, he derived nothing. At once dulled and tense, he was quite unable to learn—his self-education, which went far, was to begin when scholastic miseries ceased.

Of that time, the *Autobiography* tells us: "The indignities I endured are not to be described." And further: "I was never able to overcome—or even to attempt to overcome—the absolute isolation of my school position. Of the cricket-ground or racket-court I was allowed to know nothing. And yet I longed for these things with an exceeding longing. I coveted popularity with a covetousness that was almost mean. It seemed to me that there would be an Elysium in the intimacy of those very boys whom I was bound to hate because they hated me. Something of the disgrace of my school-days has clung to me all through life. Not that I have ever shunned to speak of them as openly as I am writing now, but that when I have been claimed as a school-fellow by some of those many hundreds who were with me either at Harrow or Winchester, I have felt that I had no right to talk of things from most of which I was kept in estrangement."

This passage was written, one must remember, by a man near the close of a wholly rewarded life. Honour, solidarity, celebrity—yes, and that lodestar of long ago, popularity—had, from middle age on, been Anthony Trollope's. He had won them; he could be modestly conscious that he deserved them. Genial and prominent figure in London clubs, "lion" guest at elegant dinner-tables, it was *he* (we may note) who was claimed as a former school-fellow by well-bred nonentities. But the longings of youth are immortal; they outlast their fulfillment. Trollope the equable, likable, bluff Victorian, on terms with (though never tainted by) his success, is a very personal figure to Trollope readers. Yet in his work there is present the outcast boy. "I longed for these things with an exceeding longing." He had fallen back, as excluded young people do, on compensatory daydreaming— "castle-building," the *Autobiography* calls it—spinning within his brain, for his own benefit, tales of valor, striking achievement, opulence, in which he was the premier actor, hero. That this engendered the story habit is obvious. As reality grew more friendly and Trollope obtained a man's proper foothold on life, he no longer needed to be his own hero. Story-making, no longer necessary as a balm, continued as a resource or spare-time activity: finally, as we know, it became his livelihood. That the early idealization did carry over, attaching itself, as the Barset novels went on, more and more to the portraiture of a certain class, the romantic-feudal peculiarities of a certain scene, was surely a factor in his pleasingness to the readers of mid-Victorian England. Even while he wrote, the world he evoked already was being shadowed by coming change, the spread of the Industrial Revolution. He clothes Barsetshire not in the melancholy of sunset but in what is, still, the mellowness of late afternoon. The Trollope "revival" in Britain, in 1940, may be accounted for by the need, then, for what Trollope could revive. He glorified what was imperilled, perhaps lost: he more than conjured up pictures, he stated a faith. Sardonic as he could be, socially critical as he was, Trollope continued to believe in "an Elysium." The belief comes right into the open in *Doctor Thorne*.

Too much has been made, perhaps, of the gloomy childhoods of subsequently highly distinguished men. I have had to lay stress on Trollope's for the following reasons. His form of early anguish is not often discussed, being depressing rather than picturesque, and even (some might consider) somewhat discreditable. The grotesque-dramatic vicissitudes of the boy Dickens, the poeticizable hardships of the Brontës, are more heard of. Had Trollope been a proletarian, he would have suffered less: as it was, he had the chagrin of feeling himself cheated of a birthright—a birthright constantly kept in view by the maniacal harpings of his father. He felt stamped by failure to make the expected grade. Then he did make *a* grade, one distinctly his own; as art, his art comes into the class of vigorous, honest conquest of disability. If the conventions within it appear cramping, one can hardly blame him: these he accepted, even throughout the years when they bore down on him. He had been the victim of a system which now, on coming into his powers, in blameless revenge he seized upon as his subject. *Doctor Thorne* is a love story, but nonetheless it involves the passions of class.

There is another factor in Trollope's workmanship—the confidence necessary for the author was built up, in him, by progress in another profession. His future, during his half-schooled, disgruntled youth, had been not the least of his mother's problems. Finally there was obtained for him, through influence, a clerkship in the General Post Office (then, as now, functioning as a branch of the Civil Service). After a phase of halfheartedness caused by boredom, mild debauchery, foolish entanglements, shiftless money troubles, he pulled himself together and did well. The General Post Office, at that time, was inaugurating throughout the British Isles a series of regional surveys, with the purpose of bettering the system; and Trollope applied to be sent, and was sent, to the south of Ireland. This, as it proved, was the turning-point—the work suited him; he found himself, overnight, a social success. Here began his foxhunting days. His salary permitted him to marry an English young lady on whom he had set his eye—and though at the start in Ireland he'd been acceptable *qua* bachelor in the numerous country houses, his popularity survived marriage. Ideal domestic happiness, and fatherhood, stabilized his emotional nature; from then on, he asked nothing more from romance. His "happy endings," when he confers them, ring true; his tongue is not in his cheek. No less important, to the man as a man, were rewarded initiative and responsibility: the Post Office acted on his reports. The to-be novelist profited by the Irish sojourn: romantically alien, unmarred for him by any saddening association, the country of crumbling mansions and twisting byways was alive with potential characters and stories. Begotten in Ireland, Trollope's earliest novel was *The Macdermots of Ballycloran,* which, taken on by his mother's London publishers, in 1847 "failed most absolutely. I never heard of a person reading it in those days." A year later *The Kellys and the O'Kellys* met a still worse fate: "The book was not only not read but was never heard of."

However, he had written them. And meanwhile the Post Office continued to nurse what it had created: reasonable self-esteem. After Ireland came a similar assignment in south-west England.

I spent two of the happiest years of my life at that task. I began in Devonshire; and visited, I think I may say, every nook in that county, in Cornwall, Somersetshire, the greater part of Dorsetshire, the Channel Islands, part of Oxfordshire, Wiltshire, Gloucestershire, Worcestershire, Herefordshire, Monmouthshire, and the six southern Welsh counties. In this way I had an opportunity of seeing a considerable portion of Great Britain, with a minuteness which few have enjoyed. And I did my business after a fashion in which no other official man has worked, at least for many years. I went almost everywhere on horseback. I had two hunters of my own, and here and there, where I could, I hired a third horse. I had an Irish groom with me—an old man, who has now been in my service for thirty-five years; and in this manner I saw almost every house—I think I may say every house of importance—in this large district. The object was to create a postal network which should catch all recipients of letters. . . . I was anxious for good results. It is amusing to watch how a passion will grow upon a man. During those two years it was the ambition of my life to cover the country with rural letter-carriers. . . . Our law was that a man should not be required to walk more than sixteen miles a day. Had the work to be done all on a measured road, there would have been no need for doubt as to the distances. But my letter-carriers went here and there across the fields. It was my special delight to take them by all short cuts; and as I measured on horseback the short cuts which they would have to make on foot, perhaps I was sometimes a little unjust to them.

All this I did on horseback, riding on an average forty miles a day. I was paid sixpence a mile for the distance travelled, and it was necessary that I should at any rate travel enough to pay for my equipage. This I did, and got my hunting out of it also. I have often surprised some small country postmaster, who had never seen or heard of me before, by coming down upon him at nine in the morning, with a red coat and boots and breeches and interrogating him as to the disposal of every letter which came into his office. And in the same guise I would ride up to farmhouses, or parsonages, or other lone residences about the country. . . .

In the course of the job I visited Salisbury, and whilst wandering there one mid-summer evening round the purlieus of the cathedral I conceived the story of *The Warden* —from whence came that series of novels of which Barchester, with its bishops, deans, and archdeacon, was the central site.

This piece from the *Autobiography* needs no comment. Here was the ideal education: practical, topographical, social. Had Trollope been travelling for a whim, at random, he would probably not have taken in half so much. Seeing the fascination of his work for the Post Office, one can understand his reluctance to quit its service—nor did he do so for years to come. Gratifyingly recognized, promoted, he carried out missions which, wide in scope, were sometimes diplomatic in nature. The rough sea voyage during which *Doctor Thorne* came to birth marked Trollope's embarkation on one such mission—he had been sent to Egypt to negotiate a treaty with the Pasha for the conveyance of British mails overland through that potentate's country. For the main, and major, part of his life, he carried on two professions concurrently, valuing his trusts as a high official no less than his accomplishment as a novelist. To a point, his adherence to the Post Office can be put down to economic caution: literary earnings fluctuate, salaries do not. But also, there was something in the duality. He enjoyed operating in two fields—the more for having, once, had no field at all.

That golden midsummer evening in Salisbury was golden in its results. *The Warden* (having been preceded by a third total failure—a historical novel, *La Vendée*) was Anthony Trollope's "first success." That is, it had notices in the press; it was read, it was talked about, and it sold—if modestly. In the writing of the more capacious *Barchester Towers,* Trollope admits he "took great delight." The work, he tells us, succeeded much as *The Warden* had succeeded—that is, "it achieved no great reputation, but it was one of the novels which novel readers were called upon to read." Together, the two books created an expectation—a readiness, even eagerness, to hear more of Barchester, county capital, and of Barset, county. Trollope, perhaps not uncleverly, kept his public waiting while he delivered himself of *The Three Clerks*, a novel largely drawn from his days of servitude, which introduces big-wigs in the Civil Service. Then, timed to the moment, came *Doctor Thorne.*

The three other, later "Chronicles of Barset" were to be *Framley Parsonage* (1861), *The Small House at Allington* (1864), and *The Last Chronicle of Barset* (1867). As their publication dates indicate, these were spaced out between various different novels, with other settings. The favour the Barset series found with the public was cumulative, growing with each volume. Trollope, however, awards the

best-selling laurels to *Doctor Thorne,* third in the
set of six. Why, in that case, did he receive (as
shown by his close accounts) £3,000 for *The Small
House at Allington,* and again £3,000 for *The Last
Chronicle,* and no more than £400 for *Doctor
Thorne?* True, the two others were magazine-
serialized, prior to publication in book form, whereas
Doctor Thorne appeared in book form only. But
Trollope's small gains from his most widely read
novel were, in fact, a penalty: he had outsmarted himself. Not yet sure of his talent, anxious for money
down, he had put a day when he was in transit
through London to what he (then) considered excellent use. Banging his way into the publisher's office,
he sold the *Doctor Thorne* copyright—outright!

I I

Almost no novel, to my mind, has a more unfavour-
able beginning than *Doctor Thorne.* Without an ink-
ling of something better to come, few readers could
stay the course of the first two chapters. Today, on
the strength of the book's reputation, we just suffer
them. The Victorian reader, supposedly, was inured
or at least resigned to this kind of prosiness—long-
winded explanation, categoric descriptiveness, and a
trend to aggressive generalization. Trollope gave himself over to every fault, from the point of view of an
"opening," that the present-day novelist schools himself to avoid. His technique, in this instance, might appear to be nil. By contrast, we are reminded of Dick-

ens's openings, vivid, immediate, dramatic, concrete;
of Thackeray's instant command of our thoughts and
will; of the Brontës' sounding out, from the very first.
Trollope wrote fast, but moved into action slowly.
Struck, himself, by this, he catches our eye disarm-
ingly at the conscientious beginning of Chapter Two:

> I quite feel that an apology is due for beginning a novel
> with two long dull chapters full of description. I am per-
> fectly aware of the danger of such a course. In so doing I
> sin against the golden rule which requires us all to put our
> best foot foremost, the wisdom of which is fully recognised
> by novelists, myself among the number. It can hardly be
> expected that anyone will consent to go through with a
> fiction that offers so little of allurement in its first pages;
> but twist it as I will I cannot do otherwise. I find that I
> cannot make poor Mr. Gresham hem and haw and turn
> himself uneasily in his arm-chair in a natural manner till
> I have said why he is uneasy. I cannot bring in my doctor
> speaking his mind freely among the big-wigs till I have
> explained that it is in accordance with his usual character
> to do so. This is unartistic on my part, and shows want of
> imagination as well as want of skill. Whether or not I can
> atone for these faults by straightforward, simple, plain
> story telling—that, indeed, is very doubtful.

Those last words, so modest, are disingenuous.
Our author, knowing what he was doing, did not
doubt his ability to do it. Straightforward story-telling
exerts a spell; Trollope could well rely on that—he,
himself, no less than ourselves, being under its power.
He takes a risk, he admits, in unloading facts before
rousing curiosity—the better procedure might be to

withhold knowledge till there has been created, within the reader, a genuine appetite to know. But the risk is justified. Foe though he was to revision or blue-pencilling, he would not have left his opening chapters to stand were their effect likely to be disastrous—or, still more, if they had lacked function. Unaware of technique (as we think of it), he had method. Essential to the interest of *Doctor Thorne* is its complex preliminary lay-out. It was necessary to establish, without ado—or, shall we say, with what seemed the minimum of it—the topography of Greshamsbury and its neighbourhood, the agricultural nature of Barset county and the political bias that went with that, and not only the identity but the status of each of his central characters, and their consequent social relationships with each other. Gradations are part of the subject of *Doctor Thorne*—spin the plot love may, but not in a vacuum: does it ever? Though Trollope wrote for mid-Victorian English readers who took the social hierarchy for granted, certain special matters needed to be explained—for these were to be factors in his story. (The Thorne family's being more ancient in origin than the Gresham, and therefore by pedigree ruling "better," is an example: hence the balance of power between Mr. Gresham, the landed squire knit by marriage into the aristocracy, and Thorne, the free-lance dispensary doctor with nothing to live upon but his earnings.)

Nor was this all. The main *Doctor Thorne* characters—the doctor and his niece, the squire and his

heir, the new-rich railway contractor Scatcherd—
gain, immensely, in interest by being within the grip
of what one might call an inherited situation. There
have been stories before "our" story opens. No one
of those stories is finished; each runs its course, still,
through its influence on the present drama. Conse-
quently, each had to be imparted, in the nearest
Trollope could find to foreshortened form. The
scandalous secret attaching to Mary's birth, her father's death at the hands of her mother's brother, and
the stigma left by the vengeance on the avenger:
these, unknown by our heroine, are her background,
her likely disqualification, her unjust handicap. The
decline in the Greshams' fortunes, still more its cause,
and with that their desperate objection to the heir
Frank's romance, demand to be analyzed and accounted for. No less, the blood-tie (of which both are
ignorant) between deplorable Scatcherd and ador-
able Mary must be, and is, prominent in the reader's
consciousness—it colours, makes complex, and deep-
ens our idea of them both.

Trollope's notion was this: that the reader should
start by knowing more about every one of the characters than any one of them knew about themselves.
(As to this, be it said, there is one exception: all-but
omniscience is granted to Doctor Thorne. On the
strength of his having to carry such dire weight, the
good man is designated the novel's "hero.") Once all
was known, the story could be set going, with the certainty of its producing the full effect. In slamming

down at us, outright, all information, Trollope was in his own way adroit—he saved himself innumerable pauses which otherwise might have been necessary along the way. Also, from now on there were needed in *Doctor Thorne* no major flashbacks into the past. When we do find the author retracing his steps, it is to account for the sayings or doings of some character who has, for the time being, been lost to sight. One admires his conscientiousness in this matter—he had a large cast to keep in play, and a devious series of doings to chronicle.

Doctor Thorne is, thus, a novel without mystery—mystery either circumstantial or psychological. We are as clear as to the character of the characters as we are to their circumstances and likely destinies. Yet the interest relies, and successfully, on suspense. How does the author achieve suspense while discarding any support from mystery? That he succeeds in doing so seems the more remarkable when one sees that his plot (or rather, his brother's) does not rely, for excitingness, on outside events—other, possibly, than the East Barset elections. No burning house, train wreck, robbery, or cataclysm of Nature is introduced; the action springs, as it ideally should, out of the characters. The predicaments which continue to grip our interest are caused by the persons who must endure or surmount them. I suggest that the magnetism of *Doctor Thorne* resides in its author's power to keep us watching. We watch, and intently, the central characters to see how they will behave in the face of circumstance, how they will react to each new development—being what they are, feeling as they must. We are present at a series of "revelations," each one producing a strong reflex: it is the reflex that we enjoy watching, though the actual matter is no surprise to us. In fact, the suspense-interest in *Doctor Thorne* is due to the author's system of keying up, gratifying, and then renewing (at still higher tenor) our expectations. The tale is a lengthy, pleasing progression from one to the next of a series of "key" scenes— each one, by its force and after-effect, being guaranteed to beget another.

In principle (though not always, I think, in practice) a preface is read before one turns to the story. In principle, therefore, it is out of order for the preface to give away the plot, or make known, by comment or discussion, the way in which the central crisis is solved. In this case, Trollope does literally "a tale unfold," and I should hesitate, even apart from scruples, to attempt to compress, into any paragraph, what by nature is leisurely and expansive. But the main situation, with which I would connect the "idea" of the novel, is another matter. I repeat my belief that it was the idea, in the first place, which fired Trollope, inspired his handling of the plot, and eventuated into this masterpiece. The idea would seem to be, a finding of levels. In the story, the characters are as it were passing each other on a staircase; some going up, some down. By the end, each person has come to a stop where he or she belongs; that is, at his or her right level—or, say, due level. What, in each case, *is* the right and the due is determined by virtue, integrity, moral character—or by the lack of them, where descents occur. Yet *Doctor Thorne,* as a story, by no means exalts the humble and meek. The hardworking country doctor and his penniless niece are, Trollope tells us outright, animated by pride—but it is a right pride. The weak squire, whose heir Frank courts Mary Thorne, fails to stand up against his overweening wife: Lady Arabella Gresham, an earl's daughter, is actuated by wrong or false pride, in which she is one with her relatives, the De Courcys. Sir Roger Scatcherd fails in the pride which should have rewarded his life's work; he sinks into squalor and alcoholism, and his son is to die of an inherited taint. The *Doctor Thorne* story indicts the abuse of privilege, the misuse of power, and the failure to be worthy of position—whether an achieved position, such as Scatcherd's, or an inherited one, such as the squire's. There is one idealized figure: good Doctor Thorne.

Trollope's ideal was this gentleman: uncompromising, "speaking his mind freely among the bigwigs," unmercenary, fearless of the conventions (he shocks other doctors by mixing his own medicines), taking his stand wholly upon integrity—an integrity backed, as his creator reminds us, by awareness of honourable and ancient lineage. For such a man, a nagging problem of conscience could not but be created by Scatcherd's will, with its possible benefit to his niece Mary; by such a man, the battle against the

Greshams, his former friends, on behalf of Mary could not be fought without sadness, regret, reluctance. The doctor despises pretension, honours tradition. Taken all in all, he realizes, I imagine, Trollope's sense of what a man not only should be but also could be. As a "hero" he must have been more rewarding than Trollope can have ever been to himself, in dark days of solitary castle-building.

This hero exhibits what might be called the outstanding, best democratic qualities. Yet he is rooted in, and subscribes to, a society in character oligarchic. His figure depends for its true proportion on being seen within the frame and against the background of the English class system of Trollope's day and the doctor's. Puzzling or even shocking as that system may seem to American readers, it demands to be accepted, or at least recognized, for the duration of the reading of *Doctor Thorne*. A work of fiction, if worth reading at all, is entitled to its own landscape, its own climate, which may often be social no less than physical. Why, after his miserable schooldays, it may be wondered, did Trollope not react against a system under whose pressures he had suffered? He was, clearly, neither poor-spirited nor subservient. But equally, he had not anywhere in him the makings of a dissident or a revolutionary; by temperament he was a romantic conformist. He was a born admirer, and the existing order provided him with much that he could admire—that he *had* admired, even when he had no part in it. The figure ideal and absolute in its independence was, to him, the gentleman. He looked no higher; in fact he would have denied that there could be anything higher at which to look.

In so far as there is class conflict in *Doctor Thorne*, it is between the country gentlemen and the aristocracy—the latter represented by the De Courcys. There is no doubt where Trollope's sympathies lie; also no doubt, alas, that his antipathies misdirect his pen. The De Courcys, a tribe of caricatures, are portrayed with uneasy, facetious venom. Negligible as villains, they fail as comedy. As elements in the novel, their chief importance is their detrimental effect on the Gresham fortunes; and to their detestable influence is traced the squire's loss of prestige among fellow-gentry and the ban upon the romance between Frank and Mary. Frank's long line of sisters, the Miss Greshams, live in peril of spinsterhood, for they dare take no mate discountenanced by their De Courcy cousins.

Barsetshire, the novel's landscape and setting, speaks for itself. This mellow county, by now so vivid to many that it becomes "fictitious" in name only, may be taken to be a sort of abstract, or compost, of those south-west English counties travelled by Trollope, on horseback, in those "happiest years" when he rode around for the Post Office. Somerset, Dorset, Wiltshire, would be three which contributed very largely; though who knows if there were not an intake, too, from the east of Devon, the west of Gloucestershire? Generically, the scene is rural-

English—wooded, rolling, with here and there a sculptural open skyline, small rivers meandering in the valleys, in which are sheltered also contented villages. Round the turns of lanes, at the heads of avenues, approached by bridges or set in orchards or ploughlands stand, great or small, the dwellings Trollope recalled—solitude their character, age their story. To the Englishman home again from uncanny Ireland, this sedate tapestried richness would have been speaking; so, after the Irish slither to ruin, would the pretty prosperity of the villages. Plotting his letter-carriers' courses, measuring byways, walking his horse on field-paths, he had come to knowing such regions like the palm of his hand; psychically it became his property.

Part of the livingness of Barsetshire is its susceptibility to change. Clouds and sunshine, summer and winter, alternate over the strong trees and the rich furrows. And in the year when the story opens, 1854, "progress" is already showing its suspect hand. Young squire-to-be Frank Gresham's coming of age is, in the scale and character of its celebration, a degree less feudal than was his father's. A Radical is among the candidates at the East Barset parliamentary elections; the Gresham-headed Tories are on the wane. Also, this is the age of railway expansion—prosperity is following the steel tracks; the coaching roads and their hostelries are left desolate. Small towns (such as Courcy, at the gates of the castle) and are askance, muted, and high-and-dry.

And how changed has been the bustle of that once noisy inn to the present death-like silence of its green court-yard! There, a lame ostler crawls about with his hands thrust into the capacious pockets of his jacket, feeding on memory. That weary pair of omnibus jades, and three sorry posters, are all that now grace those stables where horses used to be stalled in close contiguity by the dozen; where twenty grains apiece, abstracted from every feed of oats consumed during the day, would have afforded a daily quart to the lucky pilferer. . . .

Oh, my friend! my poor lame friend! it will avail nothing to tell thee of Liverpool and Manchester; of the glories of Glasgow, with her flourishing banks; of London, with its third million of inhabitants; of the great things commerce is doing for this nation of thine! What is commerce to thee, unless it be a commerce in posting on that worn-out, all but useless great western turnpike road! There is nothing left for thee but to be carted away as rubbish—for thee and many of us in these now prosperous days; oh my melancholy, care-ridden friend.

Our lame and care-ridden friend should have lived to laugh! For a hundred years have brought the wheel to full circle. "All but useless," today, stretch the steel tracks, soon to be torn up, grass sprouting between them as insolently as it did in the inn courtyard. That courtyard, a car park, again booms. The great western turnpike road is all but invisible under streaming traffic.

One final word as to the topography. Salisbury, though the first of the Barset novels was there conceived, is not to be identified with Barchester. Smaller Wells, further to the west, also claims a connection with *The Warden*. One may take it that Barchester, like the terrain surrounding it, is a compost—more truly *like* an English cathedral city than any one real-life example could hope to be. Fictitious places take on something from the at once simplifying and concentrated imagination which has created them—one may notice a sort of poverty in the atmosphere of a scene which the novelist has no more than "copied." In creating places, Trollope, one may be certain, worked as do others in his craft—that is to say, he instinctively found it necessary to add, snip, accentuate, modify, blend.

I I I

Doctor Thorne we have designated a love story. It follows the fortunes of two young people on their difficult way to achieving union. Like other novels of this kind, it has one disadvantage: we part from the (now) happy pair at the church door. We are denied a glimpse of them in the expanded relationship of marriage—and indeed throughout the course of the story we have had but too few glimpses of them in anything but a fleeting harmony. Kisses are snatched, idyllic moments are interrupted—perpetually they are in an atmosphere of emergency, or taking part in hurried councils of war. The Greshamsbury Hall attitude to the love affair is more than obstructive, it is militant. There is considerable reason on the Gresham side: Trollope admits the objections to the match, though he does not ask the reader to share them. Frank is the heir to embarrassed property; if he follows his heart and marries the doctor's niece, the Greshams *as* Greshams will have to be written off. They are faced by what, virtually, is extinction—that of a landed family shorn of land.

Oddly enough, Trollope's divided sympathies do not detract from the virtue of *Doctor Thorne*. He has built up, thanks to his plot, a first-rate predicament, from which, with a patience allied with consummate skill, he goes on to extricate his characters. Were the scales too heavily weighted on either side, the tension would be less. Emotion is kept in balance against realism— and one must grant that no one scene in the book offends, in its content, against either. Love *is* to conquer all: but exactly how? Is it a fault that, quite early in the novel, you and I, the omniscient readers, see light ahead? Economic relief is to come from the Scatcherd quarter. Roger Scatcherd killed off by alcohol, only his sickly son stands between Mary and a large fortune. Louis Scatcherd's rate of drinking himself to death must be timed against the rapidly mounting pressure piled up against Frank and Mary's love. How the race is to finish we do not doubt—throughout the lengthy final part of the book we are working to a foregone conclusion. Yet the excitement is never less.

Trollope sets and keeps burning in *Doctor Thorne* a fire no less formidable for being innocent. He creates in Mary a woman whose temperament is focussed upon a single devotion: Frank is the love of her life, there can be no other. Admirably, he matches Mary with Frank—boyish, wayward, naïvely the prey of vanity, but capable (as his adherence to Mary shows) of a sublime obstinacy, of courage, of a contempt for circumstance. Originally, Mary retreats from Frank, out of a dread of involvement—too much is at stake for her; she foresees disaster. She doubts—and one cannot wonder—that Frank is serious. They are of the same age (twenty-one, when the story starts), but he is a boy, she is a woman. Finally, after an all but speechless mutual declaration, it is to be she who involves him—part, she suggests, they must; but they know they cannot. Trollope's touch on sexual love is tentative, awkwardly light, but unfailing—true. There are present in this blameless obstructed courtship the elements of a fatal illicit passion. Behind Mary's agonized offer of renunciation, towards the end, we feel the dire force of her character—she believes her letter likely to *be* the end. If we do not share her suspense, before Frank's reply, it is because we know that he cannot leave her. Once, he had been the happy type of young man who falls out of love as painlessly as he falls into it. But Mary is a woman who is not parted from.

The attractiveness of the doctor's niece may account for the eager reception of *Doctor Thorne*. Her effect on the Victorian reader may have been not unconnected with shock tactics: she was far from being the heroine then in fashion, limp with sweetness, pulpy with femininity. She is, in fact, a heroine in the greatest English tradition, from Shakespeare on— high-spirited, witty, resourceful, graceful and debonair. She is fearless, like Fielding's Sophia; she laughs and sparkles like Jane Austen's Elizabeth (if not quite so brightly); she is as vehement, as implacable, as outspoken with regard to her own feeling as Charlotte Brontë's Jane Eyre. She has the merit of being not a person one is ever called upon to be wholly sorry for. In her relationship with her two friends Beatrice Gresham and Patience Oriel, there is a touch of teasing, flirtatious gallantry—one delights in the scene where she kisses Beatrice's toe. She is proud; in that greatly her uncle's niece. She has grown up as the playmate of the Gresham children, daily in and out of the great house; her attitude to Greshamsbury Hall is untinted by over-gratitude or subservience—in this, she could not be more unlike the put-upon Fanny in *Mansfield Park*. Banished, after her fall from favour, she sustains her position without loss of face.

Mary Thorne's character has a darker inverse. It may be that we like her the better for suspecting that she is not naturally "good." Scatcherd, coarse and tormented, is (as we always remember) her other uncle. To her birth there attaches something worse than the stigma of illegitimacy—she is not to be called a love-child; she was the fruit of an outrage committed upon her mother. Our most revealing, and constant, view of Mary is in her companionship with her doctor uncle: an equalitarianism of tender confidence. In the scenes between them, Trollope is so much at his best that *Doctor Thorne* could twice over be called a love story.

IV

The large-sized canvas of this novel is crowded around the edges with minor characters. Many owe their existence to sub-plots only; and, touched in hastily and to formula, they are for the most part no more than "types." An outstanding exception is Miss Dunstable, the plain but delightful heiress proffered to Frank by his aunt the countess in hopes of diverting him from Mary. We could do with more of Miss Dunstable than we are given; in her own right she is a major character, cramped for space by an inadequate role—though, with her affectionate shrewdness as to Frank, she is twice over permitted to act importantly: she compels him to see himself as he is, and she re-steels his will with regard to Mary. Also, there are present in *Doctor Thorne* two persons prominent in the plot but imperfectly realized psychologically. Lady Arabella Gresham and Roger Scatcherd both of them demand to be on a scale of which Trollope, in their instances, was incapable. He perceives them, but still as aliens; he fails to cope with them. Both of them, though for exceedingly different reasons, are largely beyond the bounds of his understanding. One wishes that he could have leased them out to other novelists better equipped to handle them—Lady Arabella to Balzac, Scatcherd to Dostoievsky. In extenuation of Trollope it must be said that his shortcomings were not peculiar to him: nineteenth-century French and Russian novelists were better than their contem-

poraries in England in dealing with either aristocrats
or tormented and difficult states of soul.

Trollope's disapproval of the De Courcys, of whose
stock she came, starts him off with a bias against Lady
Arabella. In the face of that, he tries hard to do moral
justice to the proud, ambitious, but far from heartless
woman—Doctor Thorne's unbending, satirical, yet
clement view of Her Ladyship may be taken to be that
of our author. In the case of Scatcherd, what does
Trollope suggest as the cause of total disintegration?
This former stonemason, after a term in prison, has
raised himself by sheer engineering genius: his rewards are abhorrent to him, all he does turns to dust.
Scatcherd once killed a man, the friend of his youth—
that he did so in vengeance, on behalf of his sister,
cannot dislodge the horror from his mind. Is it to justify Scatcherd (at least in part) that Trollope causes
his heroine Mary Thorne to have been begotten in an
atrocious manner? Scatcherd, due to play a large later
part in the story, clearly could not be allowed to go to
the gallows; at his trial, he had won the sympathy of
the court, hence his being convicted of manslaughter,
not murder. It may be feared, however, that Trollope
had yet another reason for representing the mother
of Mary Thorne as the unwilling victim of an enormity. Having failed to lure the girl from the path of
virtue, Henry Thorne (the doctor's worthless young
brother) had drugged her unconscious, then gone on
to take possession. Thus, though sinned against, the
unfortunate Mary Scatcherd still could be seen as sin-

less—"pure" as to all but fact. Trollope, one must suspect, thought this better—thus his heroine did not originate from a stoop to folly! That the way in which he accounts for her antecedents would be far more repulsive to us, he did not foresee.

Nothing changes more than the notion of what is shocking. At more than one juncture in *Doctor Thorne* we may, today, charge the author with blind spots, timid shiftiness, ethical ambiguity. The second brotherly vengeance in the book is Frank's horsewhipping of Moffat, the fashionable tailor's son who has jilted one of the Gresham sisters. (Moffat, rich, had been a De Courcy protégé.) As to this scene, we feel Trollope himself uneasy: he resorts to a rhetorical facetiousness which makes the pages in question all but unreadable, apart even from their unpleasing content. Frank, he tries hard to persuade himself, should be "manly"—we see the Gresham heir transformed (though briefly) into a fascist bully. Trollope, the mid-Victorian, was writing at a sort of transition point: behind him lay the unself-conscious rumbustiousness of the eighteenth century; ahead, a new world of scruples and sensibility. Fielding or Smollett could have got away, forthrightly, with the whipping scene, and still not offended us—Trollope wavers with regard to it, so is lost. This ambivalence of his was not, probably, evident to his early readers, for they shared it. His judgments, his acceptances, his solutions, with so very often their hint of compromise, are—where they show the hint of compromise—of his day. Frightened by abnormality in his youth, he breathed joyously the air of what seemed normality. Such deceptive air is not breathed in without a cost. He pays the cost in his art; we must see him pay it even in this his accepted masterpiece, *Doctor Thorne.* Yet somehow there remained, and remains, within him a creature of untouched, inveterate honesty. Such was the Trollope who has survived his day, the Trollope whom we consider now.

The question of artistry comes last. The idea of a novel's being a work of art not only never occurred to Trollope but would have been totally foreign had it done so. The production of novels was an industry which he found himself happily able to carry on. How far this industry was rewarded, not only afterwards by cash but at the time by release and pleasure, his *Autobiography* never exactly tells us. He appends a list of his books, their dates, and the sums gained by them; into creative sensation he does not enter. Like all authors, he thought more highly of some of his novels than he did of others; sometimes the public agreed with him, sometimes not. He worked to the clock, so many pages a day—a fact which, revealed by the *Autobiography,* was one cause of his absolute disrepute with a later, aesthetic generation. The *Autobiography,* by his expressed wish, was not published till one year after his death: he died in 1882. It is conceivable, indeed he faced the fact, that towards the end of his days he was less in fashion; he had not to live to witness his total banishment—"ordinary" readers reacted, almost at once, to the cold wind blowing upon his name. That disgrace was temporary; it is a thing of yesterday. Anthony Trollope has reappeared. He is not merely back where he was; that would be impossible, for the world he first stood in relation to is no more. The twentieth century, having discovered that it requires him, calls him back. Inevitably, we rate what he has to give us in our own terms—which are not, and cannot be, exactly his.

Speed and space-filling were the desiderata. He could not afford to be at a loss for a word; nor was he —the necessary words rushed in. (He stresses the writer's need for habituation.) He was grateful to any word so far as it served to help to establish a fact, add an attribute, or define a meaning—and "help," I think, is here the correct verb: Trollope's words back one another up, bear one another out, and, collectively, do what has been desired. That there could be fewer of them did not worry him. Fining down, selection, would have demanded a concentration of which he was not capable—or, one had better say, a concentration he did not choose to apply. Take care of the sense, and the style will look after itself, could have been his axiom. He is intelligible; he makes point after point, though the reader's arrival at each may be laborious. Like all regular day-to-day writers, he shows great variation in his degrees of command and clearness: one is aware of his better days, and his worse ones—the worst to be said about his prose is, it lacks that precision we call distinction. As against that, his dialogue can be excellent; sufficiently clear-cut, dramatic and yet lifelike—this is borne out in all the important chapters in *Doctor Thorne*. The diversionary interludes are feebler, marred often by careless conventionality, or the facetiousness we have noted before. Why, we may ask, are such interludes here at all?—often they cast no light on the central story. Answer, Trollope deliberately fought a delaying action. *Doctor Thorne* was planned as a "three-decker" (a three-volume novel). This form in his day was popular, and sold best. *The Warden,* he had decided, would have done better had it been bulkier. *Doctor Thorne* had to be spun out to the required length, and was. Inspiration could flag in him, but invention never. He was what he claimed to be, an unceasing worker.

Yet there can, I believe, be an artistry which is inadvertent—more than unconscious, all but unwilling. To this Trollope was subject; one is aware of its unmistakable action in *Doctor Thorne*. I spoke, at the outset of this preface, of his scenes' having a certain glow and rotundity; and there are moments when they have more. Something idyllic, if not poetic, is added to their intense likeliness; they become, if never piercingly beautiful, more nearly beautiful than is most reality—and when this happens there is a momentary transparency in his dense prose, as though by some magic the verbal sand reached a heat where it could run into glass. Elsewhere, at crises of emotion between the characters, that emotion not only commands us but austerely seems to command him, giving anonymous authority to his pen. An artist transmits more than he knows: in that sense we find Trollope to be an artist. On a level below that, he is a great conveyor of that to which he greatly reacted: charm —whether of face, person or manner, landscape, the visage or environment of a house. Aesthetically and fondly he loved girls, bevying in muslins, swinging their bonnets by the ribbons, dispersing over lawns liquid with sunset. He depicts floating pleasures, whose spell is in their evanescence, their slipping by. Had he been a painter, he would have been an inland Boudin. Also he took pleasure in masculine upright bearing and open countenance. Honour was his darling; grace, where he was concerned, went with strength in reserve or courage in play. *Doctor Thorne* as a novel has sterling merits—some I have touched on, others you will discover. But it acts on us most, perhaps, through some inner quality that only a warm and gentle word can define. It endears itself to us. For many, this is enough.

ORLANDO *

VIRGINIA WOOLF'S *Orlando* was first published in London in October of 1928. I remember, the book was regarded with some mistrust by one generation—

* *Orlando,* by Virginia Woolf. New York: Signet Classics, New American Library; 1960.

my own, at that time "the younger." We, in our twenties during the twenties, were not only the author's most zealous readers, but, in the matter of reputation, most jealous guardians. Her aesthetic became a faith; we were believers. We more than admired, we felt involved in each of her experimental, dazzling advances. Few of us (then) knew the still-conservative novels of her first period; a minority had informed itself of *The Mark on the Wall* and *Kew Gardens,* hand-printed and issued in 1919 by the original Hogarth Press. She broke full upon us, it would be correct to say, with *Jacob's Room,* 1922, on which followed *Mrs. Dalloway,* 1925; then, while we were still breathless, *To the Lighthouse,* 1927. What now, what next? Next came *Orlando.* It was *Orlando*'s fate to come hard on the heels of the third of those masterpieces, of which each had stimulated a further hope. We regarded this book as a setback. Now, thirty-two years later, I wonder why this should have been so.

One trouble was, I imagine, our peculiar attitude to this writer's art. Defending it as we did against all comers—"stupids," dissidents, or the unseeing critic —we were ready, should so desperate a need arise, to defend it against the artist herself. Never had we foreseen that we might require to. The virtue of the art was, for us, its paradox: sublimating personality into poetry, it had, as art, the chastity of the impersonal. Before we had read *Orlando,* indeed for some time before it was "out," we scented the book as a transgression. Unofficial publicity was unfortunate, the more so because it was unofficial. This *Orlando*—we did not care for the sound of it. The book was, we gathered, in the nature of a prank, or a private joke; worse still, its genesis was personal. Inspired by a romantic friendship, written for the delectation of the romantic friend, it was likely to be fraught with playful allusion. Nor was that all—a distinguished, sympathetic, and "special" coterie had contributed to the invention known as *Orlando*. That Virginia Woolf should have intimates was a shock.

Most of us had not met Virginia Woolf; nor did we (which may seem strange) aspire to. She did not wish to be met. Her remoteness completed our picture of her, in so far as we formed a picture at all. Exist she must (or writing could not proceed from her), but we were incurious as to how she did. What she looked like, we had not a remote idea; authors' photographs did not, then, ornament book jackets. Our contentment with not knowing Virginia Woolf today would appear extraordinary, could it even be possible. We visualized her less as a woman at work than as a light widening as it brightened. When I say, "She was a name, to us," remember (or if you cannot remember, try to imagine) what a name *can* be, surrounded by nothing but the air of heaven. Seldom can living artist have been so—literally—idealized.

Malevolent autumn of twenty-eight—it taunted us with the picture of lady given to friends, to the point of fondness, and jokes, to within danger of whimsicality. Ourselves, we were singularly uncoordinated, I see now, as generations go. When I hear it said, as sometimes I do today, that Virginia Woolf's reputation was built up by a sophisticated coterie, I ask myself: "Whom can they possibly mean?" We, the ardent many, were rank-and-file provincials, outlanders, free lances, students (to me, in 1922, reading *Jacob's Room,* Bloomsbury meant University College, London). We ran, if into anything, into floating groups, loose in formation, governed by vague affinities. Then scorning fringes of coteries, we have remained, I notice, unwilling to form their nucleus in our later days—not, I hope, hostile, but non-attachable. Nevertheless, what we heard of *Orlando* galled us. We were young enough to feel out of it.

What we loathed was literary frivolity. So this was what Virginia Woolf could be given over to, if for an instant we took our eye off her—which, to do us justice, we seldom did. Cloak-and-dagger stuff. The finishing touch was the success the book enjoyed with our elders—*Orlando* charmed its way into the forts of middle-aged folly. "Your Mrs. Woolf has so often puzzled us. But *this* book of hers is delightful! We see what you mean!" Betrayed. . . .

We, naturally, read *Orlando.* We knew neither how to take it nor what to make of it; it outwitted us. Up to this year, I had never read it again.

The position as to *Orlando* has now changed. Or, better, the book itself has a position it lacked before—

it belongs to what is central and main in the writer's work, instead of appearing, as it once did, to hover on the questionable periphery. There has been time, since Virginia Woolf's death, to stand back and view her work as a whole—still more, to see the whole as a thing of structure (in so far as an artist's whole art is like a building) or of inevitable growth (in so far as a whole art is like a tree). Though what does one mean by "a whole art"? Seldom does a writer lay down his pen or a painter his brush with calculated finality, saying: "This is forever; I have done!"

Death, other than in very old age, is an arbitrary interruption, the snipping of a cord at what seems often a fortuitous point. Rather, in Virginia Woolf's case, say her achievement within her fifty-nine years of life seems more, rather than less, significant now that we judge it steadily, *as* a whole. Up to 1941—that is, while she was living and at work—judgment was bound to be piecemeal, book by book. Temporary mists, misprisions, prejudices, sometimes intervened. From those mists' evaporation nothing she did gains more than *Orlando*. That *Orlando* was beautiful nobody doubted: what we now see is that it is important —and why.

It was important to the writer. She was the better, one feels certain, for writing it; in particular, for doing so when she did. More irresponsible than the rest of her work in fiction, it has the advantage of being less considered and more unwary. This book corresponds with a wildness in her, which might have re-

mained unknown of—unless one knew her. This was
a rebellion on the part of Virginia Woolf against the
solemnity threatening to hem her in. *Orlando* is,
among other things, rumbustious; it is one of the most
high-spirited books I know.

Personal memories of Virginia Woolf cast, for me,
their own light upon *Orlando,* though I certainly
never spoke to her of the book, heard her speak of it,
or attempted to find my way back to it while I knew
her. Friendship with her—chiefly laughter and pleasure, and an entering, in her company, into the rapture caused her by the unexpected, the spectacular,
the inordinate, the improbable, and the preposterous
—filled out nine years of the lengthy interval between
my first and second readings of *Orlando*. From her I
learned that one can be worse than young and foolish;
for she was the epitome of the young and foolish; it is
among the glories of *Orlando* that it is in some ways a
foolish book. It is not disorganized—on the contrary,
it is a miracle of "build"—but it is rhapsodical. Halfway through her creative life, she desired a plaything—
also a mouthpiece. Shyness is absent from *Orlando;* in
what sometimes are rhetorical exclamations, sometimes lyrical flashes like summer lightning, she voices
herself on the subjects of art, time, society, love, history, man, woman. The book is a novelist's holiday,
not a novel.

By definition, *Orlando* is a fantasy. What is that?
A story that posits "impossible" circumstances and
makes play with them. Fantasy may juggle with time

and space, and ignore, for instance, the law of gravity. Infinitely less fortunate is the novel, a work of imagination fettered to earthly fact and subject to dire penalty if it break the chain—one slip on the part of the novelist as to "reality" and his entire edifice of illusion totters and threatens to tumble down. At the same time, the licence accorded the fantasist is not boundless—the probable must enter his story somewhere. Should it fail to do so, interest is lost. Against extraordinary events, he must balance (in some sense) ordinary, or at least credible, characters. Where would *Wonderland* and *Through the Looking-Glass* be without the prim, dogmatic lucidity of the temperamentally *un*adventurous Alice? Virginia Woolf, whom the "musts" of the novel bored, fell in without complaint with the laws of fantasy. Her Orlando—that is, her central character—though redeemed by grace, genius, and breeding from being "ordinary," is *as a character* absolutely convincing. To the change of sex, to the mysterious flight of time —centuries slipping by like months in the country— he-she reacts in a manner one cannot challenge—psychologically, all is extremely sound. And the more transitory, lesser cast are touched in, manipulated, with great adroitness. Nothing in *Orlando,* other than the outright impossible, seems improbable. Ironically, fantasy made Virginia Woolf a more thoroughgoing "straight," one might say assiduous, novelist than she was wont to be. The entire thing was a pleasure—she did not "have to"; she was out of school.

. . .

What a performance *Orlando* is, simultaneously working on amazement and suspending disbelief! At the start, a sixteen-year-old aristocrat, male, proffering a bowl of rose water to the ancient Queen Elizabeth I; at the close, a woman of thirty-six, still Orlando, under an oak tree in the moonlight, in the reign of Britain's King George V—the month October, the year 1928, the exact day probably that of the publication of *Orlando*. The change of sex took place in Constantinople, where Orlando was being ambassador, towards the end of the seventeenth century. The longing to be a poet which consumed the youth has been realized by the woman, who has combined this with giving birth to a son. Exquisite social comedy has enjoyed a run of—roughly—three and a half centuries, partly in London, partly in the great Kentish country house. The Victorian age has been survived. Love has seared its way into a young breast, never to be forgotten, always to be associated with a Jacobean Thames ice carnival lasting a winter. Among the series of grand effronteries with which *Orlando* handles English history, there appear to be a few inadvertent errors—surely St. Paul's Cathedral acquires a dome sooner than it did? The enormous sense of release that runs through the book is partly an affair of effortless speed, mobility, action—carriages dashing, whips cracking, mobs swaying, ice islands twirling doomfully down the river. By contrast, I remember Virginia Woolf—back to being a novelist, writing *Between the Acts*—coming down the garden path from her studio, saying: "I've spent the whole of the morning trying to move people from the dining-room into the hall!"

I have a theory—unsupported by anything she said to me, or, so far as I know, to anyone—that Virginia Woolf's writing of *Orlando* was a prelude to, and in some way rendered possible, her subsequent writing of *The Waves,* 1931. Outwardly, no two works of fiction could be more different; yet, did the fantasy serve to shatter some rigid, deadening, claustrophobic mould of so-called "actuality" which had been surrounding her? In *To the Lighthouse* (coming before *Orlando*), she had reached one kind of perfection. This she could not surpass; therefore, past it she could not proceed. In *Orlando,* delicacy gives place to bravura, to rhetoric. It was a breaking point and a breathing space at the same time, this fantasy. She returned to the novel, to *The Waves,* with—at least temporarily—a more defiant attitude to the novel's "musts."

Captive in the heart of the book *Orlando,* in the midst of the splendid changing and shifting scenes, are accounts of the sheer sensation of writing, more direct than this writer has ever given us. For instance:

At this moment . . . Orlando pushed away her chair, stretched her ams, dropped her pen, came to the window, and exclaimed, "Done!"

She was almost felled to the ground by the extraordinary sight which now met her eyes. There was the garden and some birds. The world was going on as usual. All the time she was writing the world had continued.

138

"And if I were dead, it would be just the same!" she exclaimed.

There is a touch of hallucination about "reality"; creative Orlando was right, so was his-her creator. Virginia Woolf's vision conferred strangeness, momentarily, on all it fell on; it was, I believe, her effort to see things as they were apparent to *other* people that wore her down. The bus, the lamp-post, the tea-cup—how formidable she found them, everyday things! Nothing of an ordeal to her, however, were melodrama or panorama—she was at home with, or within, either.

Orlando, about which we who were then young were so stupid in 1928, is, I perceive, a book for those who are young. How does it strike those who are young now?

NORTH AND SOUTH *

North and South is a drama, a novel based upon contrasts, conflicts, and oppositions. These go down through the make of the story, layer below layer, the most apparent being the least profound. It may be that no other of Mrs. Gaskell's works so reflects the alternatives in her own nature—the principles she embraced, the recoils she felt, her sensuousness, her wakeful morality. Published just less than a hundred

* *North and South,* by Mrs. Gaskell. London: The Chiltern Library, John Lehmann; 1951.

years ago, *North and South,* like a landscape under an altered light, today presents unforeseen contours. For the contemporary reader, the accents fall on what was most instinctive, least calculated. Outdated, remote as a social document, the book stands nobly out as a work of feeling—as such it speaks; as such it should be discussed.

The North-South opposition exists in every country, however small; and, still more, has a psychic significance which cuts down deep in many of us. It seems that the North moves South; we flee South before it. Eternally, the South woos and the North repels. In reverse, the South is decadent and the North effective. Why else should the American Civil War, in the decade after the publication of this English novel of Mrs. Gaskell's, have brought, for the English imagination, so many emotional issues to a head? Mrs. Gaskell, conceiving her heroine and her hero, in effect confronted a Southern lady, formidable in pride but instinct with grace, with a stalwart Yankee for whom grace was suspect. Margaret Hale and John Thornton are prototypes; their author's uncertain genius, from time to time, quickens them into passionate sentient characters. These two are opponent-lovers, masking a mutual desire with hostility, feeding the hostility with misunderstandings—like Elizabeth Bennet and Darcy, like Jane Eyre and Rochester, like their run-down breed of descendants with whose spun-out quarrels Hollywood has delighted us long enough. It was not, however, Mrs. Gaskell's pur-

pose to write yet another love story boned on pride
and prejudice. Margaret Hale and John Thornton
play their parts as embodiments of the wider forces
contending in *North and South*.

The author's personal destiny hinged, like that of
her heroine, on a move to the industrial North. Elizabeth Cleghorn Stevenson, beautiful London girl with
a fastidious, innocent taste for pleasure, fell in love
with and married the Unitarian minister Mr. Gaskell
and went to Manchester with him to share his life
and work, to bear their children and write her stories.
For her, the transition was softened off by elation,
faith, and personal happiness. With Margaret Hale,
we have the whole shocking impact which her creator
either was spared from feeling or did not permit herself to feel: the "Milton Northern" (Manchester) of
North and South smokes up, overpowering soul and
senses with its lightless ugliness, human harshness,
and—it seems—virtual inhumanity. We are shown it
through the eyes of a dismayed girl, high in spirit as
she is fine in feeling. Margaret, bound to silence, is
the displaced person—neither love nor vocation has
brought her here; she is the victim (as one would see
it now) of her father's selfish self-abnegation. Mr.
Hale, till lately a clergyman of the Church of England
and incumbent of a pleasant living in Hampshire, has
fallen prey to "doubts," upheaved himself and his
family and come North to Milton, to make his way as
a tutor to *nouveaux riches* industrialists or their sons.
John Thornton, already into his thirties, crosses the

Hales' threshold as the first pupil. His humility with regard to culture does not atone, in the Southern lady's view, for his arrogance in regard to success, power, and wealth, his preoccupation with mastery, his contempt for the amenities which, for the Hales, are as precious as life itself.

Here is a study of two-sided social prejudice, and something more—a sort of race-antagonism. Difficult is it to realize how few hundred miles separate Hampshire and "Darkshire," London and "Milton." Mrs. Gaskell's feminine genius again appears in the way she has steered clear of generalities, pinning the central, Milton part of her story to three domestic interiors—the Thorntons', the Hales', and the Higginses'. With this third point of her triangle, the working-class Higginses, she has been least convincing; which is ironic, for they claim human priority. Justified anger, unjustifiable suffering, frustration—what is this but the inverse of the Thorntons and their Milton success story? The turbulent father and dying daughter remain (it may be found) stock figures: our author is open to the reproach of having written outside her range. But, did she? At its most nearly perfect, her art is narrow; but it could not be hermetic—its edges crack with the force of her convulsive, passionate sympathies. She failed in "presenting" the Higginses; she never failed to feel them. Moreover, they have been used, with a certain slyness, to expose the small limitations of Margaret Hale, who, in her calls in the role of ministering angel, is so often dumbfounded, or disconcerted, made aware of falseness, shrewdly put in the wrong.

The plot of *North and South* has been so contrived as to serve the theme of the story. The theme is well served; we must condone the plot. Mrs. Gaskell wrote, and wrote for a living, at a time when length (which we count as tedium), suspense, and elaboration were in demand. She employs several creaking devices which the novel might be better without, and her resorts to coincidence are, it is true, outrageous. Two or three of her "strong" scenes—notably the riot during the strike and the scuffle at the suburban railway station—should perhaps have been left to take place off-stage. All the same, when the plot is stripped for examination, its artifices begin to excuse themselves—none is there for no reason; few have failed to advance the psychological movement of the story, to illumine character, or to charge up emotion. Mrs. Gaskell, in her simplicity, conceived an ambitious, vast, and exceedingly complex picture: for this her imagination was (I contend) sufficient, her intellect less so, and her technique not. Was she not, however, in her way adroit? Visually minded, quick to convey sensation, aware of the greatness of small things, she was able to space out, throughout *North and South,* moments which not only flood the rest of the book with light but impress on it her special sense of proportion. They are moments, often, of solitude, of reflection or retrospection: in each of them may be felt her delicate strength, and their effect is to deflect the eye of mind from her stretches of more perfunctory writing. She is perfunctory where she fails to be fully present in heart, taste, fancy, and wit—she could not, perhaps, transcribe what she could not somehow enjoy, or invent (or, at least, with any conviction) experience which could not have been her own. Should, indeed, the author of *Wives and Daughters,* of *Cranford* and *Sylvia's Lovers,* have withheld her pen from scenes of guilt and misery? Such was not, and never had been, her wish. Before *North and South* had come, in the Chartist year, *Mary Barton, a Tale of Manchester Life,* then, later, *Ruth,* that plea for a fallen woman. The tender, the shrewd, the delicious, were not enough; it was imperative for her to combat wrongs.

One would insult Mrs. Gaskell were one to ignore, or dismiss with smiling indulgence, her humanitarian crusades, her moral aims. She has been grouped, with George Eliot, among the "social" novelists of her day: she would have desired and she deserves that place. To us, *North and South* must appeal upon other grounds—as a novel of manners, a precise and peculiarly fearless study of class feeling, and a work of what is from time to time an almost voluptuous sensibility. The class struggle touched on, and most truly, is of a nature almost forgotten now—the stand made by the fiercely declining gentry against "trade"; that is, the new-rich commercial middle class. Wealth, other than that derived from long-owned lands, had by association come to be a reproach; and Mar-

garet, posed like an icicle in the Thorntons' drawing-
room, finds confirmation on every hand of her innate
idea that the rich are vulgar. With the Higginses she
is, at least in intention, happy. Margaret's forlorn but
unbending hauteur is, for some reason, her not least
attractive trait. Mrs. Gaskell endows her young
heroine with a sort of muted physical splendour, a
nerve and poise which endear. Nor, in view of her
general failures with men, has the author done badly
with John Thornton. Love interest is powerful and
direct.

The richness of this novel is in its contrasts; the
North is framed by the South; the stony city is shadowed by quivering memories of trees. Helstone, the
parish in the New Forest, is the scene of the story's
first part, the tormenting ghost of its second. To Helstone, Margaret, at eighteen, returns from London,
with expectation of living her youth out here. "It was
the latter part of July . . . The forest trees were all
one dark, full, dusky green; the fern below them
caught the slanting sunbeams; the weather was sultry
and broodingly still. Margaret used to tramp along by
her father's side, crushing down the fern with a cruel
glee, as she felt it yield under her light foot and send
up the fragrance peculiar to it—out on the broad com-
mons in the warm scented light, seeing multitudes of
wild, free, living creatures, revelling in the sunshine
and the herbs and flowers it called forth." This image
her senses carry, for three years, through nightmare
Milton streets, through the shoals of (it seems) en-

slaved workers. Yet, truce is to be made, peace is to be found, the dream of the forest is to evaporate. Among the later pages of *North and South* comes Margaret's return to Helstone, with an old friend of the family: change, she finds, has been at work even here—beloved trees have been felled, old cottages swept away. " 'Yes!' said Mr. Bell. 'It is the first changes among familiar things which make such a mystery of time to the young; afterwards we lose the sense of the mysterious. I take changes in all I see as a matter of course. The instability of all human things is familiar to me; to you it is new and oppressive.' " And late that night, at the village inn, Margaret sits by her open window, "gazing out on the purple dome above, where the stars arose and twinkled and disappeared behind the great umbrageous trees before she went to bed. All night long, too, there burned a little light on earth; a candle in her old bedroom, which was the nursery with the present inhabitants of the parsonage until the new one was built. A sense of change, of individual nothingness, of perplexity and disappointment, overpowered Margaret. Nothing had been the same; and this slight, all-pervading instability had given her greater pain than if all had been too entirely changed for her to recognise it."

"There's no turning back; the path is overgrown," cries out Chekhov's Trofimov, in *The Cherry Orchard*. "If the world stood still, it would retrograde and become corrupt," rather more painfully reflects Margaret. She is to lower one flag only to raise another. In *North and South,* the characters not only face their destiny; they in the end salute it. It may be the greatness of the book that one feels within it the irresistible movement of a tide.

STORIES BY KATHERINE MANSFIELD *

I

IF Katherine Mansfield were living, she would this year be sixty-eight.† Is this fact out of accord with our idea of her? Sometimes it may be that an early death so fixes our image of a person that we cannot envisage him as older. Youth comes to seem an attribute of the personality—in the case of a beautiful woman or romantic artist, both of which Katherine Mansfield was, this happens particularly often. Yet in the case of Katherine Mansfield it becomes particularly wrong. For one thing, we lose much and deny her something if we altogether banish her in imagination from the place she could have had in our own time. For another, she had no desire whatever to be "spared" life or anything further it could bring. Useless as it is to lament her going, let us not forget she would have stayed if she could, and fought to do so with savage courage.

* *Stories by Katherine Mansfield,* selected by Elizabeth Bowen. New York: Vintage Books; 1956.
† Written in 1956.

She could not have lived as she was; she was far too ill. To restore health, at the stage her illness had reached, would have taken a miracle—she sought one. Could that have been granted, a fresh start, one can think of few people more fitted than Katherine Mansfield to have aged without decline, ignominy, or fear. One can picture her at sunset, but not in twilight. Born with good nerve, she had learned comprehensive courage, and in a hard school. In spite of setback after setback, she was already on her way towards equilibrium. Her spirit was of the kind which does not die down. Her beauty, even, was of the enduring kind, hardy and resolute in cast as it was mysterious in atmosphere—nor need one imagine her without the peculiar personal magic she emanated: a magic still so much part of her legend. Already she was "old" in imagination—up to any age, would she not have been young in temperament?

She was drawn to old people, seeing them as victors. They stood to her for vision, and for the patience she so impatiently longed to have. (She was aware, of course, also of ancient monsters.) Is it too much to say that she envied old age, and the more so as her own hopes of attaining it grew slender? But one does not waste desire on the unlikely: her real need was pressing, and grew obsessive—she needed time, time in which to achieve "a body of work." By now, she would have had thirty-four years more. Enough? I suspect that in the extreme of her desperation she would have been content to compound for ten. There is never enough of the time a writer wants—but hers was cut so short, one is aghast. The more one salutes the fulfilment in her work, the more one is awed by its stretching promise. The perfectedness of the major pieces sets up anguish that there could not be more of them. Equally, I may say that a fellow-writer cannot but look on Katherine Mansfield's work as interrupted, hardly more than suspended, momentarily waiting to be gone on with. Page after page gives off the feeling of being still warm from the touch, fresh from the pen. Where is she—our missing contemporary?

As it was, she died in January 1923, late one evening, in her bare room in the community at Fontainebleau. One's impression, from her husband's account, is that the end when it did come took her by surprise: she had been beginning again to expect life. And from then on everything, purged of dross of falseness, was to have been different. She was thirty-four, young as a woman, as an artist at the beginning of her maturity— that is, she had entered into her full powers without being yet certain how to command them.

It is with maturity that the really searching ordeal of the writer begins. Maturity, remember, must last a long time. And it must not be confused with single perfections, such as she had accomplished without yet having solved her abiding problems. She had had throughout no guide but her own light, nothing outside to check by, no predecessor. Chekhov was her ally, but not authority. In her field, Katherine Mansfield worked by herself.

She had, when she went to Fontainebleau,

reached a crisis both in regard to life and in regard to art. She had undergone an intense revulsion against her existence as it had come to be, and against her writing as she now saw it. Conflicts and the sickness they had set up, mistrusts the sickness in turn engendered, made it all but impossible for her to go forward. Essential as it was for her to have faith, she repudiated faith based on self-deception. She had come to look on herself, and with that her work, as in danger of being rotted by unreality. She sought nothing less than rebirth.

In her journal, at the close of her final August, she puts on record her part in a conversation:

I began by telling him how dissatisfied I was with the idea that Life must be a lesser thing than we were capable of imagining it to be. I had the feeling that the same thing happened to nearly everybody I knew and whom I did not know. No sooner was their youth, with the little force and impetus characteristic of youth, done, than they stopped growing. At the very moment that one felt that now was the time to gather oneself together, to use one's whole strength, to take control, to be an adult, in fact, they seemed content to swap the darling wish of their hearts for innumerable little wishes. Or the image that suggested itself to me was that of a river flowing away in countless little trickles over a dark swamp.

. . . Sooner or later, in literature at any rate, there sounded an undertone of deep regret. There was an uneasiness, a sense of frustration. One heard, one thought one heard, a cry that began to echo in one's own being: "I have missed it. I have given up. This is not what I want. If this is all, then Life is not worth living."

But I *know* it is not all. How does one know that? Let me take the case of K.M. She has led, ever since she can remember, a very typically false life. Yet, through it all, there have been moments, instants, gleams, when she has felt the possibility of something quite other.

By October of 1922, Katherine Mansfield became convinced that there must be a miracle or nothing. She made up her mind to enter the community, to subject herself to its physical rigours for the sake of inner regeneration. The step was taken against the advice and wishes of her friends. On the eve, she wrote in her journal:

How can you hesitate? Risk! Risk anything! Care no more for the opinion of others, for those voices. Do the hardest thing on earth for you. Act for yourself. Face the truth.

True, Chekhov didn't. Yes, but Chekhov died. And let us be honest. How much do we know of Chekhov from his letters? Was that all? Of course not. Don't you suppose he had a whole longing life of which there is hardly a word? Then read the final letters. He has given up hope. If you desentimentalise those final letters they are terrible. There is no more Chekhov. Illness has swallowed him.

. . . Now, Katherine, what do you mean by health? And what do you want it for?

Answer: By health I mean the power to live a full, adult, living, breathing life in close contact with what I love—the earth and the wonders thereof—the sea—the sun. All that we mean when we speak of the external world. I want to enter into it, to be part of it, to live in it, to learn from it, to lose all that is superficial, and acquired in me and to become a conscious direct human being. I want, by understanding myself, to understand others. I want to be all that I am capable of becoming. . . .

Then I want to *work*. At what? I want so to live that I may work with my hands and my feeling and my brain. I want a garden, a small house, grass, animals, books, pictures, music. And out of this, the expression of this, I want to be writing. (Though I may write about cabmen. That's no matter.)

But warm, eager, living life—to be rooted in life—to learn, to desire to know, to feel, to think, to act. That is what I want. And nothing else. That is what I must try for.

I I

"Katherine Mansfield's death, by coming so early, left her work still at the experimental stage." This could be said—but would it be true? To me, such a verdict would be misleading. First, her writing already *had* touched perfection a recognizable number of times; second, she would have been bound to go on experimenting up to the end, however late that had come. One cannot imagine her settling down to any one fixed concept of the short story—her art was, by its very nature, tentative, responsive, exploratory. There are no signs that she was casting about to find a formula: a formula would, in fact, have been what she fled from. Her sense of the possibilities of the story was bounded by no hard-and-fast horizons: she grasped that it is imperative for the writer to expand his range, never contract his method. Perception and language could not be kept too fresh, too alert, too fluid. Each story entailed a beginning right from the start, unknown demands, new risks, unforeseeable developments. Often, she worked by trial-and-error.

So, ever on the move, she has left with us no "typical" Katherine Mansfield story to anatomize. Concentrated afresh, each time, upon expression, she did not envisage technique in the abstract. As it reached her, each idea for a story had inherent within it its own shape: there could be for it no other. That shape, it was for her to perceive, then outline—she thought (we learn from her letters and journal) far more of perception than of construction. The story *is* there, but she has yet to come at it. One has the impression of a water-diviner, pacing, halting, awaiting the twitch of the hazel twig. Also, to judge from her writings about her writing, there were times when Katherine Mansfield believed a story to have a volition of its own—she seems to stand back, watching it take form. Yet this could not happen apart from her; the story drew her steadily into itself.

All of her pieces, it seems clear, did not originate in the same order. Not in all cases was there that premonitory stirring of an idea; sometimes the external picture came to her first. She found herself seized upon by a scene, an isolated incident or a face which, something told her, must *have* meaning, though she had yet to divine what the meaning was. Appearances could in themselves touch alight her creative power. It is then that we see her moving into the story, from its visual periphery to its heart, recognizing the "why" as she penetrates. (It could seem that her great scenic New Zealand stories came into being by this process.) Her failures, as she uncompromisingly saw them, together with her host of abandoned fragments, give evidence of the state of mind she voices in anguished letters or journal entries—the sensation of having lost her way. She could finish a story by sheer craftsmanship; but only, later, to turn against the results.

Able and fine as was her intelligence, it was not upon that that she depended: intuitive knowing, vision, had to be the thing. She was a writer with whom there could be no secondary substitute for genius: genius was vision. One might speak of her as having a burning gaze. But she faced this trouble—vision at full intensity is not by nature able to be sustained; it is all but bound to be intermittent. And for Katherine Mansfield those intermittences set up an aesthetic disability, a bad, an antipathetic working condition. Under such a condition, her work abounded, and well she knew it, in perils peculiar to itself. She dreaded sagging of tension, slackening of grip, flaws in interior continuity, numbness, and, most of all, a sort of synthetic quality which could creep in. She speaks of one bad day's work as "scrappy and dreamy." Dreaminess meant for her, dilution.

Subjects, to be ideal for Katherine Mansfield, had to attract, then hold, her power called vision. There occurred a false dawn, or false start, when a subject deceived her as to its possibilities—there were those which failed her, I feel, rather than she them. We

must consider later which kind or what range of subject stood by her best, and why this may have been so.
There was not a subject which did not tax her—raising, apart from anything else, exacting problems of
treatment, focus, and angle. Her work was a succession of attempts to do what was only just not impossible. There is danger that in speaking of "attempts"
one should call to mind those which have not succeeded: one forgets the no less attempt which is
merged in victory. Katherine Mansfield's masterpiece
stories cover their tracks; they have an air of serene inevitability, almost a touch of the miraculous. (But for
the artist, remember, there are no miracles.) Her consummate achievements soar, like so many peaks, out
of the foothills of her working life—spaced out, some
nearer together in time than others. One asks oneself
why the artist, requited thus, could not have been last-
ingly reassured, and how it could have happened that,
after each, troughs of frustration, anxiety, dereliction,
should have awaited her once again?

The truth was, she implacably cut the cord between
herself and any completed story. (She admits, in the
journal: "It took me nearly a month to 'recover' from
'At the Bay.' I made at least three false starts. But I
could not get away from the sound of the sea, and
Beryl fanning her hair at the window. These things
would not *die down*.") She must not look back; she
must press forward. She had not time to form a consistent attitude to any one finished story: each stood to
her as a milestone, passed, not as a destination arrived

at. Let us say, she reacted to success (if in Katherine Mansfield's eyes there was such a thing) as others react to failure: there seemed to be nothing left but to try again.

To be compelled to experiment is one thing, to be in love with experiment quite another. Of love for experiment for its own sake, Katherine Mansfield shows not a sign. Conscious artist, she carries none of the marks of the self-consciously "experimental" writer. Nothing in her approach to people or nature is revolutionary; her story-telling is, on its own plane, not much less straightforward than Jane Austen's. She uses no literary shock tactics. The singular beauty of her language consists, partly, in its hardly seeming to *be* language at all, so glass-transparent is it to her meaning. Words had but one appeal for her, that of speakingness. (In her journal we find noted: "The *panting* of a saw.") She was to evolve from noun, verb, adjective, a marvellous sensory notation hitherto undreamed of outside poetry; none the less, she stayed subject to prose discipline. And her style, when the story-context requires, can be curt, decisive, factual. It is a style generated by subject and tuned to mood—so flexible as to be hardly *a* style at all. One would recognize a passage from Katherine Mansfield not by the manner but by the content. There are no eccentricities.

Katherine Mansfield was not a rebel, she was an innovator. Born into the English traditions of prose narrative, she neither revolted against these nor broke

156

with them—simply, she passed beyond them. And now tradition, extending, has followed her. Had she not written, written as she did, one form of art might be still in infancy. One cannot attribute to Katherine Mansfield the entire growth, in our century, of the short story. Its developments have been speedy, inspired, various; it continues branching in a hundred directions, many of which show her influence not at all. What she did supply was an immense impetus— also, did she not first see in the story the ideal reflector of the day? We owe to her the prosperity of the "free" story: she untrammelled it from conventions and, still more, gained for it a prestige till then unthought of. How much ground Katherine Mansfield broke for her successors may not be realized. Her imagination kindled unlikely matter; she was to alter for good and all our ideas of what goes to make a story.

I I I

To make a selection has not been easy. In *The Short Stories of Katherine Mansfield* (Alfred A. Knopf, 1937) we have her output: eighty-eight stories, of which twenty-six are unfinished. The first of the pieces in this collection, "The Tiredness of Rosabel," was written when she was twenty; the last completed one, "The Canary," dates from the summer before her death. The time span is, thus, fourteen years.

The dimension of this present Vintage edition limits me to twenty-six Katherine Mansfield stories—obviously there could have been more had I chosen shorter ones. I decided that to sacrifice longer stories would have been an injustice to the author, all of whose masterpieces required space.

To have left out masterpieces would, I thought, also have been unjust to the Vintage reader. Well known as may be these major stories, they cannot be read too often or known too well. Here, accordingly, are "The Little Governess," "Prelude," "At the Bay," "Bliss," "Je ne parle pas français," "The Man Without a Temperament," "The Stranger," "The Daughters of the Late Colonel," "The Voyage," "The Garden-Party," and, for all it is unfinished, "Six Years After."

Next I looked for stories to be examples of Katherine Mansfield's ways of seeing or feeling; of her satire, sympathy, or favouritisms; or of her supremacy as a story-teller. "The Modern Soul," "Psychology," "Sun and Moon," "This Flower," "Revelations," "The Young Girl," "Life of Ma Parker," "Miss Brill," "Marriage à la Mode," "The Doll's House," and, again unfinished, "The Doves' Nest" make a bid for inclusion under those headings. They may be found unequally good; one or two are not even her second-best work. But each of them, I would contend, exhibits some characteristic of hers and of hers only.

Room was left (at the cost of exclusions I regretted) for the early work, with its harshnesses, its first glints of authority, and, most interesting of all, its alternatives—what kind of writer was she to be? This, as with other highly gifted young persons, did not immediately decide itself. Writers today at their own beginning must want to see how Katherine Mansfield began, and how the themes of her future work were already like reefs under the surface. "The Tiredness of Rosabel" was the first of what were to be a succession of daydream stories: apart from its interest as that, one would hardly claim for "Rosabel" that it is better than any average story turned out today by a twenty-year-old member of a writing group. Twenty-year-old Katherine Mansfield worked unaided by friendly criticism, and without the incitement of group discussion. And recall that in 1908 the idea of writing a story *about* a daydream was in itself novel—a daring break with accepted pattern. And how many "Rosabel" tales today would have been written at all but for Katherine Mansfield? Today her influence operates at more than one remove—that is to say, students who have not read her and may know hardly more of her than her name show in their own writing an unconscious debt.

Some of my choices bring me dead up against the author's stated feeling. "I couldn't have 'The Woman at the Store' reprinted, *par example,*" she protested to her husband in 1920, when she was deciding upon the list of her stories first to appear in book form. Yet "The Woman at the Store" (date, 1912) is here. I have put it in because I like it: it shows the touch of one of the earlier, possible Katherine Mansfields who, as time went on, was to be crowded out. In this it differs from "Ole Underwood," which far more foreshadows the Katherine Mansfield the world was to come to know—"Ole Underwood" is an early "injustice" story. Both are set in New Zealand, and their flavour and vigour raise a question—could she have made a regional writer? Did she, by leaving her own country, deprive herself of a range of associations, of inborn knowledge, of vocabulary? She never did, as we know, return to New Zealand as a mature woman: it took its toll of her in dreams, broodings, and often a tortuous homesickness. New Zealand was to return to Katherine Mansfield, but not before she had travelled a long way.

"Sun and Moon" she regarded, apparently, as a lapse. This story had origin in a night's dream, transcribed while the vividness lasted. I overrule her objections to "Sun and Moon" because it epitomizes one theme of hers, almost one obsession: wrecking of illusion. The flawless, famous "Bliss" has that theme on an adult plane—yet "Bliss," for all its accomplishment, is to me one of her few disagreeable stories. In the more roughly written "The Doll's House," illusion triumphs—"I seen the little lamp." . . . Disagreeableness, a compulsive brooding upon the ugly, appears in the collection of German stories, the 1912 *In a German Pension*. Two out of that volume, "The Baron" and "The Modern Soul," are here. I do not care for them, but to have left them out would have given an incomplete picture of Katherine Mansfield. She had, though she tried more and more to curb it, a terrifying faculty for contempt.

One cannot, I think, discuss this artist's work in

terms of ordinary progress. One is, rather, aware of greatened deepening and heightening. She taxed herself more rather than less as she went on—she herself remarked the loss of her first facility. The rate at which she abandoned stories shows (apart from the dislocations of sickness) how ever more demanding her art became: at the start she had asked less of it, or it less of her. That burning gaze of hers, her vision, gained in intensity: by the end almost nothing it turned on remained opaque. Her interpretations became more searching—what was spiritually happening to Katherine Mansfield gives signs of itself in the stories, one by one. Her art followed her being's, it would seem, inevitable course. Very important indeed is the continuity, and I therefore feel it very important that the stories given be in the right time-order. John Middleton Murry, her husband, established this (as nearly as could be done) for the 1937 collected edition—departing from it, he tells us, at one point only: "At the Bay," conceived as a continuation of "Prelude," is placed by him immediately after "Prelude," though actually it was written four years later. I have, in arranging my selection, kept to the Middleton Murry order, abiding by his allowable one change.

To select is a grievous responsibility, because it involves representation also. In reducing eighty-eight stories to twenty-six, there is danger of giving untrue proportion to the "body" of Katherine Mansfield's work. Stories I have had to omit could have given further significance to those chosen—for there is no doubt that short stories by the same hand do have a bearing on one another. They enhance, they throw light on each other; together they acquire composite meaning. Also, stories fall into groups according to scene, mood, subject: each masterpiece, planet-like, has satellites. In making this Vintage choice, it becomes my business to give you no two Katherine Mansfield stories of the same kind, in order to give you as many kinds as possible. Her range was wide, and I want to stress that. How her manner varied— yes, to the point, as said, of never having hardened in *a* manner—I also want to bring to your notice. Working on these lines has entailed, alas, the isolating of almost every story from its creative surround—that is, from others which led either up to or away from it. The transitions, the subconscious links between story and story, have had to go. To be forced to disturb relationships makes one, often, more conscious of their reality.

I V

I have touched on Katherine Mansfield's alternatives: the evidences, that is, in her early stories that she could have been a writer of more than one kind. Alternations went on throughout her working life. In her letters appears a brusque, formidable, masculine streak, which we must not overlook in the stories. Her art has backbone. Her objectiveness, her quick, sharp observations, her adept presentations—are these taken into account enough? Scenically, how keen is her eye for the telling detail! The street, quay-side, café, shop interior, tea-time terrace, or public garden stand concretely forward into life. She is well documented. Her liking for activity, for the crowd at play, for people going about their work, her close interest in process and occupation, give an extra vitality to stories. Admire the evening Chinamen in "Ole Underwood," or Alice, the servant in "At the Bay," taking tea with Mrs. Stubbs of the local store.

She engraves a scene all the more deeply when it is (as few of her scenes are not) contributory to a mood or crisis. Here, at the opening of "The Voyage," are the awarenesses of a little girl going away with her grandmother after her mother's death:

The Picton boat was due to leave at half-past eleven. It was a beautiful night, mild, starry, only when they got out of the cab and started to walk down the Old Wharf that jutted out into the harbour, a faint wind blowing off the water ruffled under Fenella's hat, and she had to put up a hand to keep it on. It was dark on the Old Wharf, very dark; the wool sheds, the cattle trucks, the cranes standing up so high, the little squat railway engine, all seemed carved out of solid darkness. Here and there on a rounded woodpile, that was like the stalk of a huge black mushroom, there hung a lantern, but it seemed afraid to unfurl its timid, quivering light in all that blackness; it burned softly, as if for itself.

Fancifulness, fantastic metaphor, play more part in her London (as opposed to New Zealand) scene-setting. Less seems taken for granted. "The Wrong House" (not in this selection) furnishes one example.

Here, in a residential backwater, an unloved old woman looks out of a window:

It was a bitter autumn day; the wind ran in the street like a thin dog; the houses opposite looked as though they had been cut out with a pair of ugly steel scissors and pasted on to the grey paper sky. There was not a soul to be seen.

This factual firmness of Katherine Mansfield's provides a ballast, or antidote, to her other side—the high-strung susceptibility, the almost hallucinatory floatingness. Nothing is more isolated, more claustrophobic than the dream-fastness of a solitary person—no one knew the dangers better than she. Yet rooted among those dangers was her genius: totally disinfected, wholly adjusted, could she have written as she did? Perhaps there is no such thing as "pure" imagination—all air must be breathed in, and some is tainting. Now and then the emotional level of her writing drops: a whimsical, petulant little-girlishness disfigures a few of the lesser stories. Some others show a transferred self-pity. She could not always keep up the guard.

Katherine Mansfield was saved, it seems to me, by two things—her inveterate watchfulness as an artist, and a certain sturdiness in her nature which the English at their least friendly might call "colonial." She had much to stand out against. She was in danger of being driven, twice over, into herself—by exile to begin with, then by illness. In London she lived, as strangers are wont to do, in a largely self-fabricated world.

She lived, indeed, exactly the sort of life she had left New Zealand in hopes of finding. Writers and intellectuals surrounded her—some merely tempestuous, some destructive. She accustomed herself to love on a razor's edge. Other factors made for deep insecurity. She and her husband were agitatingly and endlessly short of money; for reasons even other than that they seemed doomed to uproot themselves from home after home. As intelligentsia, they were apt to be preyed upon by the intelligentsia-seeking sub-beau monde—types she was to stigmatize in "Bliss" and again in "Marriage à la Mode." Amid the etherealities of Bloomsbury she was more than half hostile, a dark-eyed tramp. For times at a stretch, there was difficulty as to the placing of her stories; individually, their reception was uncertain: no full recognition came till the volume *Bliss*. In England she moved, one gets the impression, among nothing but intimates or strangers —of family, familiar *old* friends, neighbours, girl-hood contemporaries, there were none. Habits, associations, were lacking also: here was a background without depth, thwarting to a woman's love of the normal. From this parched soil sprang the London stories.

To a degree it was better, or always began by being better, in the south of France. She felt a release among Mediterranean people and the Midi light reminded her of New Zealand's. It was at Bandol, late in

1915, that she began "The Aloe," original version of "Prelude," and thereby crossed a threshold. At Bandol was suffered the agony out of which the story had to be born. She had come to Bandol to be alone with loss: her brother Chummie, over with the army from New Zealand, had been killed fighting in France. His last leave had been spent with Katherine in London. That same month, late at night in her sea-facing hotel room, she wrote in her journal:

The present and future mean nothing to me. I am no longer "curious" about people; I do not wish to go anywhere; and the only possible value that anything can have for me is that it should put me in mind of something that happened or was when we were alive.

"Do you remember, Katie?" I hear his voice in the trees and flowers, in scents and light and shadow. Have people, apart from these far-away people, ever existed for me? Or have they always failed me and faded because I denied them reality? Supposing I were to die as I sit at this table, playing with my Indian paper-knife, what would be the difference? No difference. Then why don't I commit suicide? Because I feel I have a duty to perform to the lovely time when we were both alive. I want to write about it, and he wanted me to. We talked it over in my little top room in London. I said: I will just put on the front page: To my brother, Leslie Heron Beauchamp. Very well: it shall be done.

That winter, though she had other maladies, tuberculosis had not declared itself. When it did, south of France winters became enforced. War continued, the wind whistled, *volets* clattered, the Mediterranean sea turned to black iron. She burned, shivered, coughed, could not bear herself, wrote, wrote, wrote. 1919–20 brought the Italian nightmare, Ospedaletti. These weeks, months, in cut-price hotels, ramshackle villas, were twice over exile, exile with doubled force. One man's letters from London were the lifeline, and letters did not invariably come. Who can measure the power of that insatiable longing we call homesickness? Home, now she was torn from it, became hers in London. She thought of the yellow table, the Dresden shepherdess, the kitten Wingley—growing up without her. Loneliness, burning its way into Katherine Mansfield, leaves its indelible mark upon her art.

She wrote the august, peaceful New Zealand stories. They would be miracles of memory if one considered them memories at all—more, they are what she foresaw them as: a reliving. And, spiritually as in art, they were her solution. Within them fuse the two Katherine Mansfields: the sturdy soul and the visionary are one. The day-to-day receives the full charge of poetry.

And now one and now another of the windows leaped into light. Someone was walking through the empty rooms carrying a lamp. From a window downstairs the light of a fire flickered. A strange beautiful excitement seemed to stream from the house in quivering ripples.

This is the child Kezia's first, late-night sight of the Burnells' new home. Katherine Mansfield the artist is also home-coming.

V

The writer was a woman of strong feeling. How quick were her sympathies, vehement her dislikes, total her angers, penitent her forgivingness, letters and journal show. If we had not these, how much would we know of her from her stories? Impersonality cannot but be the aim of a writer of anything like her calibre, and she fought to keep her stories clear of herself. But, human temperament and its workings being her subject, how could she wholly outlaw her own? And temperament played in her work an essential part—it was to provide as it were the climate in which ideas grew and came to flower. That throughout years of her creative life Katherine Mansfield was a sick woman, and that tuberculosis engenders a special temperament, or intensifies the one there already, must be allowed for. It has been more than allowed for—there is danger, in her case as in Keats's, that the medical history be overstressed. We are to marvel at the persistent strength with which Katherine Mansfield the artist threw off the sick-room. She was conscious only of her vocation—she *was* to write, she wrote, and wrote as she did. It may be that brutalities on the part of fate made her the more feel singled out, set apart. The battering at her health accounts for the inequalities of her accomplishment: that there was any trace of the pathological in the art itself, I imagine nobody could assert.

She was not by nature dispassionate. In the New

Zealand, the "far-away people" stories, conflict seems stilled—there is an overruling harmony, the seer come to rest with the seen. Katherine Mansfield's ethics and partisanships come through far more in the English pieces (possibly because of their thinner fabric) and in some of those set in the south of France—though in "The Young Girl" and "The Doves' Nest" we again have a shining impartiality. . . . She loved right-eousness and hated iniquity: what, for her, consti-tuted those two? She was on the side of innocence and honour: honesty, spontaneity, humbleness, trustful-ness, and forbearingness distinguish characters she is fond of. No less could she embody what she detested: cruelty or heartlessness, affectation, neurotic indul-gence, cowardice, smugness. Indignation at injustice, from time to time, makes her no less inflammatory a writer than Charles Dickens. She concerns herself with bad cases rather than bad systems: political awareness or social criticism do not directly express themselves in the stories. How hard is her bearing against oppressors, how tender her leaning towards victims! Unimaginativeness, with regard to others, seemed to her one of the grosser sins. The denial of love, the stunting of sorrow, or the cheating of joy was to her not short of an enormity—she had an intense regard for the human birthright.

How good is Katherine Mansfield's character-drawing? I have heard this named as her weak point. I feel one cannot insist enough upon what she instinc-tively grasped—that the short story, by reason of its aesthetics, is not and is not intended to be the medium either for exploration or for long-term development of character. Character cannot be more than *shown*—it is there for use, the use is dramatic. Foreshortening is not only unavoidable, it is right. And with Katherine Mansfield there was another factor—her "stranger" outlook on so much of society. I revert to the restrictedness of her life in England, the eclecticism of her personal circle. She saw few people, saw them sometimes too often. This could account for her tendency to repeat certain types of character. This restless New Zealand woman writing of London deals with what was more than half a synthetic world: its denizens *are* types, and they remain so—to the impoverishment of the London stories. The divorce of the intelligentsia from real life tends to be with her an obsessive subject—aggravated more than she knew, perhaps, by her sense of being far from her home base. Her sophisticates are cut out sharply, with satire; they are animated, expressive but two-dimensional.

In the south of France stories, characters are subsidiary to their environment; they drift like semi-transparent fish through the brilliantly lighted colours of an aquarium. Here, Katherine Mansfield's lovely crystallization of place and hour steals attention away from men and women. Could *she* not bear to examine these winter visitors—idle, halfhearted, and non-indigenous? Tense Anglo-Saxons, they contrast with physically equable busy natives—beauty cheats them, Nature withholds her secret. Patient is the husband without a temperament; true is Miss Brill to her fur necktie; the young girl is a marvel of young hauteur. Yet these three, even, no more than brush one's memory: the south of France stories are about moods.

Katherine Mansfield, we notice, seldom outlines and never dissects a character: instead, she causes the person to expose himself—and devastating may be the effect. The author's nominal impassivity is telling. I should not in the main call her a kind writer, though so often she is a pitiful one. Wholly benevolent are her comedies: high spirits, good humour no less than exquisite funniness, endear to us "The Daughters of the Late Colonel," "The Doves' Nest," "The Singing Lesson." Nor is the laugh ever against a daydreamer.

The New Zealand characters are on a quite other, supreme level. They lack no dimension. Their living-and-breathing reality at once astonishes and calms us: they belong to life, not in any book—they existed before stories began. In their company we are no longer in Katherine Mansfield's; we forget her as she forgot herself. The Burnells of "Prelude," "At the Bay," and "The Doll's House" are a dynasty. Related, though showing no too striking family likeness, are the conversational Sheridans of "The Garden-Party." Of Burnell stock, graver and simplified, are elderly Mr. and Mrs. Hammond of "The Stranger"—Katherine Mansfield's equivalent of James Joyce's "The Dead." Alike in Burnells, Sheridans, and Hammonds we feel the almost mystic family integration. Husbands and fathers are convincing; men give off an imposing masculinity. These men, women, old women, young girls, children, are in a major key. I do not claim that the New Zealand stories vindicate Katherine Mansfield's character-drawing—the drawing is not (to my mind) elsewhere at fault. What she fails at in the European stories is full, adult character-realization—or, should one say, materialization? Her Londoners are guessed at, her New Zealanders known. As to the Burnells she had information of the kind not gained by conscious experience. Writing of these people, she dwells upon them—her art grew not only from memory but from longing.

The New Zealand stories are timeless. Do the rest of the Katherine Mansfield stories "date"? I find there is some impression that they do—an impression not, I think, very closely checked on. To an extent, her work shows the intellectual imprint of her day, many of whose theories, tenets, preoccupations, seem now faded. It is the more nearly *mondaine,* the "cleverer" of her stories, which wear least well. Her psychology may seem naïve and at times shallow—after all, she was young; but apart from that much water has flowed under bridges in thirty years. "Bliss," "Psychology," and "Je ne parle pas français" (technically one of her masterpieces) give out a faintly untrue ring. And one effect of her writing has told against her: it was her fate to set up a fashion in hypersensitivity, in vibratingness: it is her work in this vein which has been most heavily imitated, and travesties curdle one's feeling for the original. The idea of her as a literary Marie Laurencin, sponsor of a brood of gazelle-eyed heroines, tends too much to be a prevailing one. In fact in her verve, raciness, husky sensuous poetry, life-likingness, and sense of the moment's drama, she is more often sister to Berthe Morrisot.

She wrote few love stories; those she did today seem distant, dissatisfying. Staking her life on love, she was least happy (I think) with love in fiction. Her passionate faith shows elsewhere. *Finesses,* subtleties, restless analysis, cerebral wary guardedness, hallmark the Katherine Mansfield lovers. Was this, perhaps, how it was in London, or is this how Londoners' *amours* struck young New Zealand? She had left at the other side of the world a girlhood not unlike young Aunt Beryl's: beaux, waltzes, muslin, moonlight, murmuring sea. . . . We revert to that entry near the close of her journal: ". . . take the case of K.M. She has led, ever since she can remember, a very typically false life. Yet, through it all, there have been moments, instants, gleams, when she felt the possibility of something quite other."

The stories are more than moments, instants, gleams: she has given them touches of eternity. The dauntless artist accomplished, if less than she hoped, more than she knew. Almost no writer's art has not its perishable fringes: light dust may settle on that margin. But against the core, the integrity, what can time do? Katherine Mansfield's deathless expectations set up a mark for us: no one has yet fulfilled them. Still at work, her genius rekindles faith; she is on our side in every further attempt. The effort she was involved in involves us—how can we feel her other than a contemporary?

STORIES BY ELIZABETH BOWEN *

OFTEN, at different times, I thought I should like to select from my own stories—reread them all, evaluate them afresh. Intermittently I have been writing short stories for what, now, is more than thirty-six years: no wonder a mass of them has amounted. A selection, I felt, should act as a sort of pointer to those which could be considered the most enduring, the most lively, the most nearly good art. Those chosen should be those fit to survive—stories on which my reputation could hope to rest. Also from the first I have had my favourites, dearer, more satisfying to me than others; those, I thought, I should easily single out. The selection (this volume, as I envisaged it) was to have about it an ideality—not that any one story I had written *had* been ideal, but the best should gain, and set one another off, by being no longer crowded by lesser neighbours.

Now it comes to the point, now that I am invited to make my choice and draw up my list, it is not so simple. Choice, for instance, involves judgment; judg-

* A selection made by the author. New York: Vintage Books; 1959.

ment requires a long perspective. Can I stand far enough away from my own work? Also, there cannot but be something alarming about the finality of my own decisions: never shall I be able to appeal against them, for I made them! As I see it, this volume must "represent" my stories—as though on the assumption that those not in it are due to be blown away on the dust of time. What, exactly, do I want to have represented? What, throughout my life, have I been trying to do, and at which points have I come nearest doing it? Have I, since first I sat down to write, had always the same ideas, or have these altered?—my manner has changed, certainly. (This last is a question I have to raise, as I should with regard to the work of another author. But that is not to say that I can reply to it.) Above all, I am confronted by the question of fairness, justice—I must be fair to the writer, not less so because she has been myself; at the same time, I must do rightly by the reader. The writer pleads to be shown at her best only, the reader might prefer an "average" view. The fact is, that every short story is an experiment—what one must ask is not only, Did it come off? but, Was it, as an experiment, worth making?

What kind of stories does, or did, Elizabeth Bowen write? This Vintage volume should be the answer. Some idea should be given of the range of subjects, of the technique and its variations, of the imaginative quality, and so on. Misfired pieces, possibly, should go in, alongside those better conceived or more fully realized—as against that, why misuse space when there's not much of it? Stories to be read should be good, as good as they can be: here, even the best show cautionary errors to any student of writing who cares to look for them. I have decided to face criticism by offering stories which certainly do invite it, but which also should, in their ways, stand up to it. These eighteen pieces (the earliest written when I was twenty) can claim to be fair examples of themes and treatments. No, to be candid, though I say "fair" examples, these are the most hopeful I can produce. If I had written better stories, they would be here.

Not only—now that I settle down to my task—do I confront problems; I sustain disappointments. A number of favourites, for instance, have played me false, failing under the test of austere rereading. I must have cared for them, I can only think, for some subjective or associative reason, long since evaporated. Alternatively, they were (unbeknownst to me) synthetic; not pure in origin, but inspired, rather, by some intellectual fashion or aesthetic caprice—many of them were written some time ago; because they were of their day, in their day they pleased me. When I was young—and youth in a writer lasts—I was easily impressed; it appears now that there were moments when I impressed myself. Sad as it is, several "favourites" were among my first discards. What were they but mirages in my memory? I fancied them better than they were.

Equally, I find that I reject stories which reek to

me of myself, by exhibiting sentiments—or, betraying them. In some, I do not seem to have been enough on guard. Such stories seem overwritten, or, still worse, yoked to my personality. I am dead against art's being self-expression. I see an inherent failure in any story which fails to detach itself from the author—detach itself in the sense that a well-blown soap-bubble detaches itself from the bowl of the blower's pipe and spherically takes off into the air as a new, whole, pure, iridescent world. Whereas the ill-blown bubble, as children know, timidly adheres to the bowl's lip, then either bursts or sinks flatly back again.

Total impersonality in story-writing is, for me certainly, impossible—so much so that it would be a waste of time to wonder whether it would be desirable. And I doubt, actually, whether for any writer it is either desirable or possible, for this reason: the short story is linked with poetry, and that, we know, cannot but bear a signature. The tale without lyricism or passion desiccates into little more than a document. The poet, and in his wake the short-story writer, is using his own, unique susceptibility to experience: in a sense, the susceptibility is the experience. The susceptibility, equally, *is* the writer, who therefore cannot be absent from what he writes. The short story is at an advantage over the novel, and can claim its nearer kinship to poetry, because it must be more concentrated, can be more visionary, and is not weighed down (as the novel is bound to be) by facts, explanation, or analysis. I do not mean to say that the short story is by any means exempt from the laws of narrative: it must observe them, but on its own terms. Fewer characters, fewer scenes, and above all fewer happenings are necessary; shape and action are framed for simplification. As against that, there are dangers and can be penalties: essentially, at no point in the story must the electrical-imaginative current be found to fail. Novels legitimately have "slack" passages, which serve, like intermissions, to ease off the reader between crisis and crisis. But the short story revolves round one crisis only—one might call it, almost, a crisis in itself. There (ideally) ought to be nothing in such a story which can weaken, detract from, or blur the central, single effect.

This, I recognize, has been one idea I have kept before myself. In short-story writing it has been my main aim, and at least as an aim it has been continuous. I state it, though without deluding myself that I have realized it, succeeded in it, in any one story. . . . To return to the matter of the personal, I repeat that one cannot wholly eliminate oneself, for a second, and also sufficient, reason: any fiction (and surely poetry, too?) is bound to be transposed autobiography. (True, it may be this at so many removes as to defeat ordinary recognition.) I can, and indeed if I would not I still must, relate any and every story I have written to something that happened to me in my own life. But here I am speaking of happenings in a broad sense—to behold, and react, is where I am concerned a happening; speculations, unaccountable stirs of interest, longings, attractions, apprehensions without knowable cause—these are happenings also. When I reread a story, I relive the moment from which it sprang. A scene burned itself into me, a building magnetized me, a mood or season of Nature's penetrated me, history suddenly appeared to me in some tiny act, or a face had begun to haunt me before I glanced at it.

On the whole, places more often than faces have sparked off stories. To be honest, the scenes have been with me before the characters—it could have seemed to me, even, once or twice, as though the former had summoned the latter up. I do not feel, necessarily, that this is wrong: a story must come to life in its own order. Also, I reassert what I said when discussing the art of Katherine Mansfield: I do not feel that the short story can be, or should be, used for the analysis or development of character. The full, full-length portrait is fitter work for the novelist; in the short story, treatment must be dramatic—we are dealing with man, or woman or child, in relation to a particular crisis or mood or moment, and to that only. Though (and as to this, law is stern) the crisis must be one in which such-and-such a character would be likely to be involved, or, still more, would be likely to precipitate; the mood must be one to which such-and-such a character would be likely to be prone, or still more, to heighten; the moment should essentially be the one which would, on the given character, act most strongly. Once a story truly germinates in my mind, the inevitable actors in it take form—and not only this, but they also take hold, to the point of remaining after the tale is told. I give, as examples, four stories in this selection: "The Storm," "Her Table Spread," "Ivy Gripped the Steps," "Mysterious Kôr." Each of these arose out of an intensified, all but spellbound beholding, on my part, of the scene in question —a fountain-filled Italian garden in livid, pre-thundery light; a shabbily fanciful Irish castle overlooking an estuary; an ivy-strangled house in a formerly suave residential avenue; or weird moonlight over bomb-pitted London. Each time I felt: "Yes, this affects me—but it would affect 'X' more. Under what circumstances; for what reason? And who *is* 'X'?" In each case, the "X" I pondered upon became the key character in the resultant story. . . . It could seem to me that stories, with their *dramatis personae,* pre-exist, only wait to be come upon. I know I do not invent them; I discover them. Though that does not mean that they are easily told. On me devolves the onus of narration.

Fantasy . . . another important element. One may of course say that any story (from any pen) is the exercise or working out of a fantasy—that any author of fiction, to write at all, must have recourse to his or her dreaming faculty. But in Elizabeth Bowen stories, it may be found, fantasy is often present twice over; part as it is of the fabric of the actual plot, or governor of the behaviour of the characters. Looking through this selection I have made, I find fantasy strongly represented. Critics may possibly say, too much so? Yet these, I still maintain, are my better stories. If I were a short-story writer only, I might well seem to be out of balance. But recall, more than half of my life is under the steadying influence of the novel, with its calmer, stricter, more orthodox demands: into the novel goes such taste as I have for rational behaviour and social portraiture. The short story, as I see it to be, allows for what is crazy about humanity: obstinacies, inordinate heroisms, "immortal longings." At no time, even in the novel, do I consider realism to be my forte. Fortunately, however, there are many other writers; taken all in all we complement one another—literature is a compost to which we are each contributing what we have. The best that an individual can do is to concentrate on what he or she can do, in the course of a burning effort to do it better.

A full and considerable number of years of life, plus more or less continuous care for writing, ought not altogether go for nothing. I cannot attempt to outline my development, though I cannot believe there has been none. The fact that this Vintage volume opens with a story about a little girl reminds me how recurrent a subject, with me, have been youth and childhood. I cannot say that I see this to be "nostalgia"; for one thing, I now enjoy my own adult state. Rather I perceive how much I rely, in art, on immediacy and purity of sensation, and indubitably the young are unspoiled instruments. Many of the greatest writers of short stories, and poets, died before Time had stolen their freshness from them. I have remained in the world dangerously long: I hope there may still be something I need not forfeit.

ENCOUNTERS *

THESE STORIES, the first of mine to be published, were written when I was between twenty and twenty-three. Their arrangement is that of the first edition, 1923, as to which I was helped by Frank Sidgwick, my first publisher. The order happens to be, roughly, chronological, though I do not think either of us had that in mind.

I must have reread *Encounters* several times when the original copy reached my hands: to have failed to be dazzled by print would have been unnatural. (Not one of the stories had ever "appeared" before; all magazine editors had rejected them.) Since that summer, I had not read the collection through till I undertook this much later edition's preface. By now, I ought to be old enough to control those split, heated, or tangled feelings aroused in writers by their very early work. All the same, can I hope to approach *Encounters* as dispassionately as if these were stories by some unknown young person, sent to me for an opinion, or a review? I suppose not.

* *Encounters,* by Elizabeth Bowen. Republished, together with *Ann Lee's,* under the title *Early Stories.* New York: Alfred A. Knopf; 1951.

What I remember, chiefly, about the writing is, the newness of the sensation of writing anything. It is, of course, to be doubted whether that sensation does ever become familiar; or, still more, whether the writer ought to desire that it should. The sense of total commitment, of desperate and overweening enterprise, of one's whole self being forced to a conclusive ordeal, remains a constant. What possibly does wear off (or grow through familiarity less acute) is that first uncanny complicity with one's physical surroundings, the objects, sounds, colours, and lights-and-shades comprehensively known as "the writing-table." The room, the position of the window, the convulsive and anxious grating of my chair on the board floor, were hyper-significant for me: here were sensuous witnesses to my crossing the margin of a hallucinatory world.

Embarking upon my first story, "Breakfast" (not the first I had started, but the first that I finished), I felt this to be, somehow, a last hope. I was twenty; already I had failed to be a poet; I was in the course of failing to be a painter. My whereabouts was the top of a villa at Harpenden; an attic of which the dormer window was set high—only when I stood up could I see back gardens, apple trees, a blur of Hertfordshire country away beyond. Between the sill of the window and the top of my table intervened a stretch of cream-dotted white wallpaper, lightly mapped by damp—damp which must have filtered in through the outdoor tiling. The map, as I sat at the table, was at eye level. The short curtains, sprigged with moss roses, had often blown out into the rain; fretting over my head, they smelled slightly musty. Now and then a voice from one or other of the gardens could be heard. The main line of the (then) Midland Railway ran along the end of my aunt's road: from time to time an express roared by, or, more intrusively, a slower train rattled towards the Harpenden stop. I wrote by hand, as clearly as seemed possible—as when at school, two or three years before, I had been making a presentable copy of an essay. A bottle of blue-black ink stood in a saucer; I used a ribbed brown pen-holder with a "relief" nib. The writing block, which had cost ninepence, had lined pages: this I found an aid to clearness of thought.

The importance to the writer of first writing must be out of all proportion to the actual value of what is written. It was more difficult then than it would be now to disentangle what was *there,* there on the page, from the excitement which had given it birth. There could be but one test of validity: publication. I know I shaped every line in the direction of the unknown arbiter. When I say that had I not written with the idea of being published I should not have written, I should add that I did not so much envisage glory as desire to know that I *had* made sense. I wanted proof that I was not prey to delusions—moreover, publication was the necessary gateway to being read. I know that I wrote then with no less, though also with no more, difficulty than I do today: as an occupation writing enthralled me, which made it suspect, but also killed me, which made it in some way "right." The thing was a struggle. I saw no point in killing myself for the sake of anything that was not to become an outright reality. For me reality meant, the books I had read—and I turned round, as *I* was writing, from time to time, to stare at them, unassailable in the shelves behind me. (This was my room, containing most things I owned.) I had engaged myself to add to their number.

To retreat upon the short story, when one is a poet *manqué,* is today a decision frequently made. In my youth, the short story's position was more anomalous. It had not yet, I think I am right in saying, been recognized as "a form." There had been, so far, little constructive-critical interest in the short story's inherent powers and problems. Or were there any such interest, I did not know of it—I could not have been further out of the movement. I had not gone to a university; I formed part of no intellectual group or aesthetic coterie. I read widely, but wildly. I did not know the stories of Hardy or Henry James; I had heard of Chekhov, but no more. I had not read Maupassant because I dreaded the bother of reading French. . . . Katherine Mansfield was not only to be the innovator but to fly the flag; since *Bliss* the short story had been more prominent. I first read *Bliss* after I had completed my own first set of stories, to be *Encounters*—

then, exaltation and envy were shot through, instantly, by foreboding. "If I ever *am* published, they'll say I copied her." I was right.

Did I, then, in writing my early stories, imagine I was doing something without precedent? Not quite. I had come on examples, which were incentives—Richard Middleton's *The Ghost Ship,* E. M. Forster's *The Celestial Omnibus.* Both I had read at school.

The *Encounters* stories are a blend of precocity and naïveté. Today, they do not seem to me badly written; the trouble with some may be, they were not well found. But at twenty—twenty-one, twenty-two, twenty-three—where is one to turn? Stories require people (*other* people). At that age one is bound up in one's own sensations—those appear to be new; actually, what is new is one's awareness of them, and one's pleased cultivation of that awareness. Literature, in those particular years, excited me according to its power to reflect, express, magnify, and give body to states of feeling of which I came to be conscious in myself. Also, it would not be too much to say that my attitude to literature was brigandish; I could not wait to rifle its vocabulary. I was at the pupil stage, too glad to be shown anything that I had not seen. I perceive, now, how in the *Encounters* stories I was making use (at times) of synthetic language to express what *was* real and true to me none the less.

To do myself justice, I was clever in my way of using a story as a device—partly framework for, partly justification of, what I did care truly to gaze upon, or

what interested me. The characters in the stories—
are they no more than stand-ins, or impatiently
jerked-at marionettes? To them, I appear ungratefully
harsh. It is the harshness, the quickness to show up,
or score off, those helpless *Encounters* "characters"
which today displeases me. Were they called into being to be made mock of? *Encounters'* author was not
so much adolescent as an instance of overprotected
childhood. . . . It seems worth remarking (*a*) that
with very few exceptions—the child in "Coming
Home," the schoolgirls in "Daffodils," Laura in "Sunday Evening"—all these men and women were senior
to myself, involved in experiences I did not wot of,
often gutted by passions beyond my ken: and (*b*) that
not more than three of them bore resemblance to anybody met in my (then) brief life. They all the more
impressed me, I do remember, by having a "real-
ness" for which I could not account. They came it
over me, even while I stuck pins in them, by wearing a badge of maturity which was none of mine.

I feel that I had a snobbery with regard to age. For
my generation, grown-ups were the ruling class. As an
only child I had lived very much among them, noted
as closely as possible their habits, and filed what appeared to be their ideas. Motherless since I was thir-
teen, I was in and out of the homes of my different
relatives—and, as constantly, shuttling between two
countries: Ireland and England. I was, it seemed, at
everyone's disposition. Though quite happy, I lived
with a submerged fear that I might fail to establish

grown-up status. That fear, it may be, egged me on to writing: an author, a grown-up, must they not be synonymous? As far as I now see, I must have been anxious to approximate to my elders, yet to demolish them. At the same time, I was not yet ready to try conclusions with any world I knew. My story characters, therefore, lived in houses which, in life, I had no more than glimpsed from the outside.

So far, social motive. Dislike of myself being at a disadvantage may have caused me to take it out on my characters at a disadvantage, to snapshot them at a succession of moments when weakness, mistrust, falseness, were most exposed. But, one point more: in fairness to the writer of *Encounters* one must allow for intellectual fashion, and for the psychological climate of a decade. The now famous Twenties, aseptic and disabused, had already set in, though without a name. If I was *mal elevée* in my attitude to the human race, so were my betters.

The *Encounters* stories have build, style, and occasional felicities of expression which I must say I like. They have a striking visual clarity; and though there may occur "conscious" phrases, sense and feeling seldom bog down in words. And I find in the best of them something better—an attempt to say something not said before. "Daffodils," "Requiescat," "All Saints," "Mrs. Windermere," "The Shadowy Third," "Sunday Evening," and "Coming Home" claim my respect. As a performance, "The Return" is the most showy, but it has a hollow kernel—a situation I must have thought up, rather than felt. A ring of emotion issues from "Coming Home"—which in fact was transposed autobiography. "Requiescat" and "The Shadowy Third" make me, now, clearly see how I used to work: I would posit a situation and then explore it. A more malignant example of that method is, "The Evil That Men Do—."

I was still not clear, while writing *Encounters,* as to the difference between a story and a sketch. I did not grasp that, while it could be emancipated from conventional "plot," a story, to be a story, *must* have a turning-point. A sketch need not have a turning-point, for it is no more than extra-perceptive reportage. ("Breakfast" and "The Lover" are examples.) When one or two 1923 book reviewers spoke of *Encounters* as "a collection of sketches," I felt that to be derogatory. It would have been right to describe the volume as "a collection of sketches and stories." Today, I imagine, few writers, now at the age that I then was, would have a similar blind spot—story-consciousness has gone on maturing.

I claim for *Encounters* one further merit—susceptibility to places, particular moments, objects, and seasons of the year. This shows itself with the naïveté of a natural love. "Daffodils" overflowed from remembered pleasure in the streets of St. Albans one sunny March afternoon; "Requiescat" released an obsession about Lake Como, and a terraced garden through whose gates I had peered. Even in the too ambitious "Return," I see the genuine love for the emptiness of an empty house; and the setting, if not people, of "The Shadowy Third" seems to be given frame by emotion. One reason to spring on my characters at their trying moments—their susceptibilities were, then, at the pitch of mine.

I was indebted for the publication of *Encounters* (had it not been published, what would have happened next?) to three persons—an older friend, the "M.J." of the dedication, who paid for having the stories typed; Rose Macaulay, upon whose verdict as to whether I was or ever could be a writer I hung my future; and Frank Sidgwick, to whom Rose Macaulay wrote. He not only encouraged me by his confidence, but made my most exorbitant dream come true by issuing *Encounters* in the same format as that of *The Celestial Onmibus*. And the title, to which my collection owed much, was of his finding.

ANN LEE'S *

ANN LEE'S, again a collection of short stories, my second book, was published in England in 1926. The actual date of the stories is earlier by a year or two; some were written while *Encounters* was still in press. And in the pause between the completion and the appearance of *Ann Lee's* I wrote my first novel, *The Hotel*.

Encounters had had a better reception than I had dared hope. How far this might be due to the book's

* *Ann Lee's*, by Elizabeth Bowen. See note on *Encounters*, p. 182.

format, and to its place in a series of known distinction, I had enough realism to ask myself. To the critics in 1923 I record my gratitude. I had envisaged being ignored; I had braced myself to meet snubs; most of all, I had dreaded patronizingness. As it was, I received what I most wanted: judgment. Looking back at that year, I perceive what good reviewers were then in the field. By goodness in a reviewer I don't mean kindness, or the predisposition to let beginners off light; I mean, readiness to search for potential quality in the work of a writer not known before—with which must go insistence, as the writer continues, that he fall not short of his original mark. Up to a point, the young writer's expectations of himself need to be nurtured; only the feeling critic can guess at the desperation they have to fight. And, on his side, the young writer is not easily fooled; he can measure the perspicacity of the critic. I doubt whether praise *with* judgment ever turned a head. I cannot overemphasize the importance, to the emerging writer, of first reviews. Do I, then, argue that every young writer should be encouraged? I can only be thankful that I was.

Encounters did not sell widely. Sidgwick and Jackson must have sustained loss; for their new author their venture had been a gain, a steadying and an education. Cheered up, I also was sobered down. Promotion from amateur status carried certain alarms with it—not only the fear of disappointing, later, those who had spoken up for me, but violence of the

incentive to work again. To continue to write is as trying as to begin. Every step forward brings one into an
area of new dangers, involves a call on powers which
may or may not be there.

The first of the *Ann Lee's* stories collection was
"The Back Drawing-Room"; after that came "The
Storm." The first brought in Ireland; the second, Italy
—as did "The Contessina" (Como) and "The Secession" (Rome). Between 1923 and 1926, my assault
on magazine editors had continued—backed by the
reasonable hope that *Encounters'* good reviews might
have won me a footing. That, however, was far from
being the case: I fared hardly better than I had done
before. "Ann Lee's" itself, it is true, had the distinction of being published in *The Spectator,* in summer
1924; it was, I believe, the first short story that peri-
odical ever carried. For that experiment, I have to
thank John Strachey, who, then in charge of the literary side of his father's paper, invited me to send in a
tale. It was he, too, who urged me to go (or, rather,
resume going) to the cinema, just then emerging from
disrepute. There was much, he remarked, to be
learned from new screen technique. I in part
learned it.

In the autumn of 1924 *The Queen,* thanks to the
daring of its then editor, Naomi Royde-Smith, took
"The Contessina"; in the following year *The London
Mercury* accorded a welcome to "The Parrot," and
"Making Arrangement" came out in *Eve.* Other-
wise, silence. For editors, did I carry the mark of

Cain? Rebuffs shook my faith: *was* I writing non-sense? I became saturnine as to the sincerity of editors who professed to be searching for new talent. They still cared, it seemed, for nothing but the establishment. Always the same gang. Could a new-comer hope to break through those ranks? It appeared, not.

I do not know whether the position of a new story writer really was more difficult then than it is today. My string of failures with periodicals seemed to me, naturally, exceptional. That my work did not quite make the required grade may occur to readers. These *Ann Lee's* stories are halfway between the first bright phase of experimentation and the necessary next degree of command. They show advance, but advance at an awkward stage—the disarming, bumbling naïveté of *Encounters* is missing. Though, like the later pieces in *Encounters,* they are of an ambitiousness which deserves respect. What I regret, on behalf of myself of years ago, is not the overweeningness but the playing safe—which betrays itself, in several of these studies of human extremity and dereliction, in the small smile of one who, herself, knows better. An author should never know better than his characters. The odious superiority of young persons needs breaking down—as a rule, life arranges this soon enough. It is dismaying to find my superiority preserved forever in the amber of print.

The inhumanity of some of the *Ann Lee's* stories may be forced the more into prominence by their fair technique. The scene-setting is surer than in *Encoun-*

ters; dialogue is lively and has shape, and action (always my problem) seems under control. These pieces have more texture, body, substantiality, than their predecessors. There is less indecision: the critics, by perceiving what sort of writer I ought to be, had done much to help me direct my powers. I was, with now more deliberation, still concerned with the possibilities of atmosphere. One must recall that in the first half of the 1920's, the period in which my first books were written, the idea and potentials of "atmosphere" were accounted new. *I* had not heard of the thing till I read my notices. In trying to find words for the hazy queerness some places and a number of persons had for me, I was bona fide; I cannot accuse myself of being prey to a literary vogue. By now, much that came fresh to me has been (not by me) exploited and overused. There sets in a mistrust of what could be fuzziness. I still, however, think it would be a pity if a young person's liking for the imponderables (which, after all, are his own discoveries) were spoilt for him, or too much guarded against. One is most honest when one is most surprised; it is one's first perceptions that first surprise one.

There is a prettiness in the *Ann Lee's* stories—prettiness of hats in a shop, of a parrot on a flowering chestnut-tree, of the Contessina's juvenile muslins against a glittering lake-scene, of broken Roman brick walls—*"so solid yet with such a silver-pink bloom of impermanence."* That younger sister of beauty delighted me. I was, as to one particular, still where I was when I wrote *Encounters*—I liked scenes and inanimate objects better than people. My pen was ready enough, as the stories show, to dwell upon scenes of guilt and misery; but it was essential that the locale be pleasing, or at any rate piquant or picturesque. I found writing, though harder and harder work, to be an outlet for my frivolity—and I cannot, today, think the stories the worse for that. Had I not enjoyed them, they would have remained unwritten.

The principal *Ann Lee's* stimulus was travel: in a sense, everything I experienced *was* travel. Now that I had really become a writer, I could look back painlessly at my own past—two childhood stories, "The Visitor" and "Charity," are, I think, the most sterling in the collection. I was by now not only a writer but married, a matron, the mistress of a house. The sensation of actually *living* anywhere, as apart from camping or visiting, was new to me. We were living in the English Midlands, outside Northampton; a flat but reposing view of garden allotments stretched away almost to the horizon, outside the window in which my table was—the nearest high point, neighbours said, was the Ural Mountains. A canal-side walk inspired "Human Habitation," and the sunny tossing chestnut-tree, waxy with blossom, at the corner of our road, set off "The Parrot." I otherwise drew on the distant, rather than nearer, scene. Some days I caught a train and went to London; I visited Ireland to see my father; every spring brought me to weeks in Italy; in late summer my husband and I travelled in France.

Between journeys I worked, at the knee-hole table in the projecting window, with an uninterruptedness I might envy now.

The enjoyment of writing the *Ann Lee's* stories was in one way clouded: *should* I be writing a novel? One reviewer of *Encounters* used the phrase "these novels in miniature"; and Mr. Sidgwick was certain I had it in me. My difficulty, as I had the wits to realize, was that I could not at that time expand my vision outside the range of an incident or an hour. I could spotlight, but not illumine steadily. I could expose or surprise people, but I had little sense of their continuity: I had a flitting mind. My view, to be a view at all, had to be dramatic, and I could not see how interplay between persons could sustain itself throughout the whole of a book—might not my characters, herded too long together, begin to exhaust or bore one another?—or, still worse, exhaust or bore me? The requisite for a novel is slow combustion; and I liked flashes. This transitional difficulty into the long-term view is no doubt generic to writers who begin as short-storyists. Rereading my stories, I used to wonder whether any of them *could* have been extended: I always decided, not. Yet I saw, if adherence to the short story were to be a matter of sheer timidity, inelasticity, or stunted competence, there would be a danger of the short story's coming, one day, to deaden under my hand. I wanted not so much to write a novel as to be able to write one, if I wanted.

I don't know whether the on-the-move mood in which I wrote them has left any mark on the *Ann*

Lee's stories. Possibly it made for tenseness—livid, pre-thundery weather, as in "The Storm." Up against human unknowableness, I made that my subject—how many times? The stories are questions posed—some end with a shrug, others with an impatient or a dismissing sigh. The nameless, unexplained man in "Ann Lee's"—*"scudded across their patch of visibility. By putting out a hand they could have touched him. He went by them blindly; his breath sobbed and panted. It was by his breath they knew how terrible it had been—terrible. Passing them blindly, he stabbed his way on into the fog."* The fate of the missing woman in "The Secession" is not hinted at: nor is the lateness of Willy in "Human Habitation" ever explained. The couple in the Tivoli villa in "The Storm" —where do they go next? Yet I cannot consider those trick endings; more, it seemed to me that from true predicament there *is* no way out.

Ann Lee's was, like *Encounters,* received favourably. I wonder how, as a new book, it would fare to-day? The short story has grown up since 1926. I am glad the *Ann Lee's* stories are in existence. They are the work of a living writer whom I know in a sense, but can never meet.

THE LAST SEPTEMBER *

THIS, my second novel, was published in 1929, having been written the year before. I was still young, or at

* Preface to the Alfred A. Knopf edition of *The Last September*. New York, 1952.

least young as a writer, and, in spite of having accomplished *The Hotel,* still afraid of novels—that was, as an undertaking. Fewer alarms surrounded the short story. Now I have more experience, it appears to me that problems, inherent in any writing, loom unduly large when one looks ahead. Though nothing is easy, little is quite impossible. It was a mistake to think of The Novel in the abstract, to be daunted by its "musts" and its "oughts," to imagine being constricted by its rules. At the outset, however, one cannot but shrink from anything one feels that one should attempt yet suspects oneself of feeling unequal to. Myself I was most oppressed, in advance, by the difficulty of assembling a novel's cast—bringing the various characters to the same spot, keeping them there, accounting for their continued presence (in real life, people seemed to be constantly getting up and going away), and linking them close enough, and for long enough, to provide the interplay known as "plot." In the short story, people intersected each other's lines of fate, but for moments only. So far, the constituents of my fiction had been encounters, impressions, impacts, shocks. One can see that, generally, in the novel the characters are maintained in the same orbit by some situation which sets a trap for them—some magnetic interest, devilment, quest, or passion. My solution was a more childish one: again in *The Last September*, as in *The Hotel,* I used the device of having my men and women actually under the same roof— to remain there, whether by choice or chance, for such time as the story should need to complete its course. To the Italian Riviera hotel of my first novel succeeded the large, lonely Irish house. I am, and am bound to be, a writer involved closely with place and time; for me these are more than elements, they are actors. The impending close of "the season," everyone leaving, gives climax to the drama of *The Hotel. The Last September,* from first to last, takes its pitch from the month of the book's name.

Yet to suggest—if I have suggested?—that I came at *The Last September* as a solution of my major mechanical problem in novel-writing would be gravely untrue. This, which of all my books is nearest my heart, had a deep, unclouded, spontaneous source. Though not poetic, it brims up with what could be the stuff of poetry, the sensations of youth. It is a work of instinct rather than knowledge—to a degree, a "recall" book, but there had been no such recall before. In "real" life, my girlhood summers in County Cork, in the house called Danielstown in the story, had been, though touched by romantic pleasure, mainly times of impatience, frivolity, or lassitude. I asked myself *what* I should be, and when? The young (ironically, so much envied) all face those patches of barren worry. In my personal memory, I do not idealize that September of 1920, the month in which this novel chose to be set. But the book, not "true" (it deals with invented happenings, imagined persons), is at many, many removes from autobiography. Proust remarks that it is those very periods of existence which are lived through, by the writer or future writer, carelessly, unwillingly, or in boredom that most often fructify into art.

The Last September is the only one of my novels to be set back, deliberately, in a former time. In all others I wanted readers to contemplate what could appear to be the immediate moment—so much so, that to give the sense of the "now" has been, for me, one imperative of writing. For *The Last September,* that went into reverse—the "then" (the past) as an element was demanded. The cast of my characters, and their doings, were to reflect the mood of a vanished time. "All this," I willed the reader to know, "is done with and over." From the start, the reader must look, be conscious of looking, backward—down a backward perspective of eight years. Fear that he might miss that viewpoint, that he might read so much as my first pages under misapprehension, haunted me. The ordinary narrative past tense, so much in usage, seemed unlikely to be forceful enough; so I opened my second paragraph with a pointer: *"In those days, girls wore crisp white skirts and transparent blouses clotted with white flowers; ribbons threaded through . . . appeared over the shoulders."* Lois's ribbons, already, were part of history.

When one is young, years count for more, seem longer: to have lived through a few, even, appears a conquest. And in most lives the years between twenty and twenty-eight *are* often important, packed with changes, decisive. When I sat in Old Headington, Oxford, writing *The Last September,* 1920 seemed a long time ago. By now (the year of the writing: 1928) peace had settled on Ireland; trees were already branching inside the shells of large burned-out houses; lawns, once flitted over by pleasures, usefully merged into grazing land. I myself was no longer a tennis girl but a writer; aimlessness was gone, like a morning mist. Not an hour had not a meaning, and a centre. Also changes had altered my sense of space— Ireland seemed immensely distant from Oxford, more like another world than another land. Here I was, living a life dreamed of when, like Lois, I drove the pony trap along endless lanes. Civilization (a word constantly on my 1928 lips) was now around me. I was in company with the articulate and the learned. Yet, onward from the start of *The Last September,* it was that other era that took command—nor is it hard (now that 1928 seems as distant as 1920) to see why. The writer, like a swimmer caught by an undertow, is borne in an unexpected direction. He is carried to a subject which has awaited him—a subject sometimes no part of his conscious plan. Reality, the reality of sensation, has accumulated where it was least sought. To write is to be captured—captured by some experience to which one may have hardly given a thought.

The factual background of *The Last September*— state of affairs round Danielstown, outside happenings which impact on the story—may, for non-Irish readers, need explanation. The action takes place during "the Troubled Times"—that is, the roving armed conflict between the Irish Republican Army and British forces still garrisoning Ireland. Ambushes, arrests, captures and burnings, reprisals and counter-reprisals, kept the country and country people distraught and tense. The British patrolled and hunted; the Irish planned, lay in wait, and struck. The army lorry heard in the breathless evening, the purposeful young man glimpsed in the Danielstown woods, the shot in the ruined mill, the barbed-wire fence round the dancers, and the ambush in which the subaltern Gerald falls—these are fiction with the texture of history. In such an atmosphere, the carrying on of orthodox conventional social life (as they did at Danielstown) might seem either foolhardy or inhuman. One can only say, it appeared the best thing to do. The festivities I have pictured are authentic—they ceased, admittedly, in the more menacing 1921. Irish-British hostilities were brought to an end by the Treaty of 1922; though upon that followed the further chaos caused by the Irish Civil War.

During the Troubles, the position of such Anglo-Irish landowning families as the Naylors, of Danielstown, was not only ambiguous but was more nearly heart-breaking than they cared to show. Inherited loyalty (or, at least, adherence) to Britain—where their sons were schooled, in whose wars their sons had for generations fought, and to which they owed their "Ascendency" lands and power—pulled them one way; their own temperamental Irishness, the other. The Naylors and their kind entertained British officers because this was a hospitable tradition—see most Anglo-Irish memoirs or old-time novels. Though the custom now made for danger, or disrepute, the gentry welcomed the military, as before. But the Troubles troubled everything, even friendliness—see Sir Richard's sombre reaction to Gerald's company. Repugnant became the patrols and raids, the proclaimed intention of "holding the country down." If it seem that Sir Richard and Lady Naylor are snobs with regard to Lois's young officers, recall that the uncle's and aunt's ideas dated back to impeccable years before 1914. "The Army's not what it was"—death had seen to that! Lois's war-damaged gallants of 1920 came of less-favoured stock than had Lady Naylor's —nor could they endear themselves by enjoying Ireland: *was* this the time? Lady Naylor's ambivalent attitude to the English, in general, should however be noted; it is a marked Anglo-Irish trait.

Why was Lois, at her romantic age, not more harrowed, or stirred, by the national struggle round her? In part, would not this be self-defence? This was a creature still half-awake, the soul not yet open, nor yet the eyes. And world war had shadowed her schooldays: *that* was enough—now she wanted order. Trying enough it is to have to grow up, more so to grow up at a trying time. Her generation, mine, put out few rebels and fewer zealots. Like it or not, however, she acquiesced to strife, abnormalities, and danger. Violence was contained in her sense of life, along with dance music, the sweet-pea in the garden, the inexorable raininess of days. Tragedy, she could only touch at the margin—not Gerald's death but her failure to love. Was it sorrow to her, Danielstown's burning? She was niece always, never child, of that house.

I *was* the child of the house from which Danielstown derives. Bowen's Court survived—nevertheless, so often in my mind's eye did I see it burning that the terrible last event in *The Last September* is more real than anything I have lived through.

THE SECOND GHOST BOOK*

THIS collection, *The Second Ghost Book,* introduces ghosts of the 1950's. We treat of the modern ghost— or, at least, of the modern way of seeing one. Do ghosts, in their nature, change with the times? As a theme, they are timeless; as institutions, they have a sort of stability, of a macabre kind. Ghosts, we hope, may be always with us—that is, never too far out of the reach of fancy. On the whole, it would seem they adapt themselves well, perhaps better than we do, to changing world conditions—they enlarge their domain, shift their hold on our nerves, and, dispossessed of one habitat, set up house in another. The universal battiness of our century looks like providing them with a propitious climate—hitherto confined to an-

* *The Second Ghost Book,* edited by Lady Cynthia Asquith. London: James Barrie; 1952.

tique manors, castles, graveyards, crossroads, yew walks, cloisters, cliff-edges, moors, or city backwaters, they may now roam at will. They do well in flats, and are villa-dwellers. They know how to curdle electric light, chill off heating, or de-condition air. Long ago, they captured railway trains and installed themselves in liners' luxury cabins; now telephones, motors, planes, and radio wave-lengths offer them self-expression. The advance of psychology has gone their way; the guilt-complex is their especial friend.

Ghosts have grown up. Far behind lie their clanking and moaning days; they have laid aside their original bag of tricks—bleeding hands, luminous skulls, and so on. Their manifestations are, like their personalities, oblique and subtle, perfectly calculated to get the modern person under the skin. They abjure the over-fantastic and the grotesque, operating, instead, through series of happenings whose horror lies in their being just, *just* out of the true. Ghosts exploit the horror latent behind reality: for this reason, they prefer prosaic scenes—today's haunted room has a rosy wallpaper. Half-tones of daylight, the livid hush before thunderstorms, glass-clear dusk, or hallucinatory sunsets suit them better than out-and-out pitch-dark night. Worst of all, contemporary ghosts are credible.

Why ghosts remain so popular may be wondered. "*I* heard a ghost story, the other day," still is a way of commanding almost all conversation. Ghosts draw us together: one might leave it at that. Can there be something tonic about pure, active fear in these times of passive, confused oppression? It is nice to choose to be frightened, when one need not be. Or it may be that, deadened by information, we are glad of these awful, intent, and nameless beings as to whom no information is to be had. Our irrational, darker selves demand familiars. But then, *are* ghosts irrational? It more and more appears that they work to plan—that, remorselessly, icily, they keep an end in view. What irks them?—how are they to be placated? In the former days, Christian burial of ill-used remains, the settling of an ancient score, or the putting right of a wrong used to close the matter: now it is not so simple. Ghosts seem harder to please than we are; it is as though they haunted for haunting's sake —much as we relive, brood, and smoulder over our pasts.

Why ghosts should today be ubiquitous is another matter. Tradition connects them with scenes of violence—are we now to take it that any and every place is, has been, or may be a scene of violence? Our interpretation of violence is wider than once it was; we are aware that the blow physically struck is but one means by which man injures man, that cruelty may be worst in its mental part, that the emotions have their own scale of torment, that the most deep-going outrages may be psychological. We fear that which hath power to hurt the soul. Inflictions and endurances, exactions, injustices, infidelities—do not these wreak their havoc, burn in their histories, leave their mark? *Who* knows what has gone on, anywhere? May not obsessions stay in the air which knew them, as a corpse stays nailed down under a floor?

Most of the stories in this book hinge on obsession —though not always of a ferocious kind: two of the most innocent turn on cricket. There are cases of obsession, or will, so strong that the moment of death goes by unperceived, innocuous—the intended action pursues its course or vision continues, without a jar. There is the air-raid story, in which a love, interrupted at highest pitch, is set free to renew its claim by a charnal incident. There is the terrible, mounting reaction of a man to the house he lives in. On the whole, we come to have the impression that persons are as hauntable as places—perhaps more so. Almost all the ghosts in these stories build themselves up out of the neuroses of those who see them—as though the seers had been selected prey. Indeed, often the ghosts are nemesis—dragging buried guilt up, harping on broken faith, or driving a mortal offence home. The author tracked down by one of his characters, recurrent figure of evil in all his books, does not survive the ordeal—this, perhaps, is one of our most unnerving tales: it conveys the sense of being *closed in upon*. So does the Editor's story, in which a fear pervades a sunny room in a happy home—there is a threat of doom here, and not for nothing.

Some are in lighter vein. The girl dancing-partner, out of her grave for the evening, has about her a ballad-like quality. Some are tender: salvation sweet-

ens the end of the darkling Walter de la Mare story—
which points to the fact that ghostliness has a poetic
element. There must be, and must be conveyed, a
sense of the *strange*—unearthly expectation and apprehension can only be rendered in fairly fine terms.
Fear has its own aesthetic (as Le Fanu, Henry James,
Montagu James, and Walter de la Mare have re-
peatedly shown) and also, its own propriety. A story
dealing in fear ought, ideally, to be kept at a certain
pitch. And that austere other world, the world of the
ghost, should inspire, when it impacts on our own,
not so much revulsion or shock as a sort of awe.

Fiction is the ideal pacing-ground for the ghost—
"apparitions," when they occur in real life, are apt to
seem to lack meaning, or lack wholeness. About a
ghost one longs to be told more—and of that, research
often falls short: that, the imagination must supply.
Yet ghost stories are not easy to write—least easy
now, for they involve more than they did. We present
here, in *The Second Ghost Book,* a series of adventures and experiments: each, it may be claimed, in its
own way carries the stamp of other-reality. In our
seeing of ghosts, each of us has exposed our susceptibilities, which are partly personal, partly those of our
time. We are twentieth-century haunters of the
haunted. The subject, at any rate, goes far back.

REVIEWS

A WRITER'S DIARY *

VIRGINIA WOOLF left behind her twenty-six volumes
in her handwriting—her diary, started in 1915,
broken off by her death, in 1941. As a diary-keeper,
she was irregular. "There are," says her husband,
"sometimes entries daily for every day; more usually
there is an entry for every few days and then there
will be a gap of a week or two. But the diary gives for
twenty-seven years a consecutive record of what she
did, of the people whom she saw, and particularly of
what she thought about these people, about herself,

* *A Writer's Diary,* by Virginia Woolf. Edited by Leonard
Woolf. New York: Harcourt, Brace; 1954.

about life, and about the books she was writing or
hoped to write."

Upon Leonard Woolf the editorship of the diary
has devolved; and with that the onus of decision—a
decision more or less certain to be challenged. What
he elected to do was, to follow through the internal
continuity of the writer. That is to say, he has com-
pressed for us, into one volume entitled *A Writer's
Diary*, whatever directly refers to his wife's work.

What could have been hoped for was everything
which bore on the artist's writing; that is, her sense of
existence as an entirety. Mr. Woolf's withholding of
the bulk of the diary, on the score that it was too
personal to be published during the lifetimes of people who figure in it, has already been, if not challenged outright, queried. Something less prying than
curiosity may lie behind readers' dissatisfaction. A
diary is an inadvertent self-portrait. It is felt or feared
that the picture as now it reaches us may be lopsided;
or that the editor's judgment as to what *is* continuity
may have been arbitrary; or that the excisions sacrifice too much else to the interests of a pain-saving
caution. All such objections, it should be said, Mr.
Woolf at the start did himself foresee. He has, in
advance, done his best to answer them. "At the best,"
he declares, "and even unexpurgated, diaries give a
distorted view of the writer, because, as Virginia
Woolf herself remarks somewhere in these diaries,
one gets into the habit of recording one particular
kind of mood—irritation or misery, say—and of not

writing when one feels the opposite. The portrait is therefore at the start unbalanced . . ." His stated aim, as editor, is to correct the unbalance there might have been. As little should be out of the true as possible. One must compute the enormous difficulties of his task. He knew her; the diary, published, was to go out to thousands of persons who did not.

A Writer's Diary, as it has come to us, never shifts from its focus: the writing writer. Such, whether at work or not, was Virginia Woolf. Art was what she was for. In a case of genius, *is* being (existence) ever quite separated from its purpose? Times there may be when divorce appears to occur: in the life, irrelevancies mount up—the more agonizing because the writer both sees their nature and feels their power. The chief threat is the threat from what does not matter—hence resentment, protest, the "irritation or misery." Into the diary, Virginia Woolf discharged her fury against the consuming futile—interrupters, the overplayed social farce, persons whose inner vacuum sucked at her. Great giver out of vitality, she objected—who does not?—to being robbed of it. Who knows what we did to her, we who knew her? If the diary knows, it has kept its secret, largely. Within these selected pages, the rest is silence. And what perhaps was it but a residuum, raged against, then forgotten the day after? As a friend she was prodigal with her time and laughter, her teasing, at times her discerning pity. And no word remains in the diary that could mar that memory. Kind to us, the editor has been fair to her—for could *she* wish, through the long run of eternity, to revoke, even impair, any joy she gave? The spring of her art was one kind of joy.

The diary gives an impression of too great somberness. It does not give an impression of being stripped. It is not spare, as would be a craftsman's notebook. It is full of mood, of tempo; it registers the ups-and-downs of an impassioned relationship. Disliking to be designated "a woman writer," Virginia Woolf shows herself most a woman in the intensities, crises, panics, and exaltations with which her relationship to her art was fraught. Harmony was her happiness. In 1924, "galloping over" the revision of *Mrs. Dalloway,* she notes: "It seems to leave me plunged into the richest strata of my mind. I can write and write now: the happiest feeling in the world." To the end of her life, such moments were to recur—though between them what stretches of terror, what troughs of anguish! As one should, she mistrusted her subjectivity: "Not," she says, "that my sensations in writing are an infallible guide." Hence, no doubt, what may astound, even shock, some readers of *A Writer's Diary:* her sensitivity to criticism, her suspense till she knew the result of her book's impact on another mind. There were the phases of dejection, of dereliction, or of an alienating fatigue—"Thought of my own power of writing with veneration, as of something incredible, belonging to someone else; never again to be enjoyed by me." And there was the problem, the ordeal presented by the writer's emergence from isolation: the once solitary burner of the writing-lamp on the Richmond table found herself within a widening limelight. Appreciation by an eager few, recognition by an increasing many, fame, threatening "popularity"— book by book, the situation was to take clearer form. It foreshadowed itself as early as 1921.

Well [she then writes], this question of praise and fame must be faced. . . . How much difference does popularity make? . . . One wants, as Roger said very truly yesterday, to be kept up to the mark; that people should be interested and watch one's work. . . . One does *not* want an established reputation, such as I think I was getting, as one of our leading female novelists. I have still, of course, to gather in all the private criticism, which is the real test. When I have weighed this I shall be able to say whether I am "interesting" or obsolete. . . . As I write, there rises somewhere in my head that queer and very pleasant sense of something which I want to write; my own point of view. I wonder, though, whether this feeling that I write for half a dozen instead of 1500 will pervert this?—make me eccentric—no, I think not.

And that poltergeist of her house of the spirit, vanity!—"Poor Mlle Lenglen," she notes, "finding herself beaten by Mrs. Mallory, flung down her racquet and burst into tears. Her vanity I suppose is colossal." Was it, perhaps, latent fear of possible accessibility *through* vanity which was at the root of Virginia Woolf's contemptuous misprision of the world? "Brilliant" occasions find her derisive, hostile. All the time, though with and after each book the indicator-needle oscillated or faltered, there mounted the pressure towards success. *The Waves* brought about the height; with *The Years* a potential drop came. And then it was, most of all, that absolutely she recognized her own virtue—the untouched ice, the savage intractability of the spirit which must experiment. To please she was willing, but never to please at all costs. Never once did she do the same thing over again.

The question she raises for the reader (that is, the reader of her novels) is the question that, in one or another form, she forever poses to herself—"What is my own position towards the inner and the outer? I think a kind of ease and dash are good; some combination of them ought to be possible. The idea has come to me that what I want now to do is to saturate every atom . . . to give the moment whole, whatever it includes." This was in 1928: *Orlando* is newly glittering on the world; three major novels are still ahead of her. What appalled her, as it must still appal others of us, were the non-moments, the bridge-passages, the "narrative business of the realist: getting from lunch to dinner: it is false, unreal, merely conventional. Why admit anything to literature that is not poetry—by which I mean saturated?"

The question remains unanswered yet.

—*The New York Times Book Review*

THE GOLDEN APPLES *

WHEN one speaks of "imaginative writing," one may use the term too vaguely and widely. Fiction is often no more than *inventive* writing—the plot is found, the characters are made lifelike, the scene of the story assumes a short-term reality. All this requires, on the part of the writer, hard concentration and patient ingenuity: the result is entertainment which gives pleasure, and for which thanks should be due. But the fact that much fiction is written to formula cannot be ignored. The formula is created by the wish of the public to be told, yet once again, what it knows already, or to have the same tune played, with slight variation, on a range of feelings of which it is already aware. The inventive writer has to his or her credit a new *story,* but the ideas conveyed by (or feelings contained in) the story have been taken from stock. No new world has been created, no unique vision sheds light, nothing of significance has been laid bare. The reader, having been held for a sum of hours, agreeably, by the inventive novel or book of stories, closes the volume and puts it down again. That is that. He is, as far as he knows, satisfied—nothing disturbs him, nothing haunts him. He has been left, in fact, where he was before. Like a child automatically stretching out its hand for another bun, he heaves

* *The Golden Apples,* by Eudora Welty. New York: Harcourt, Brace; 1949.

himself out of his chair and goes to his book-table, or puts on his hat and goes to his library, in search of another work of fiction which shall resemble the one before.

If imaginative writers were more numerous, the inventive less so, there would be a less rapid turnover of fiction. The work of imagination causes a long, reflective halt in the reader's faculties. It demands to be reread, to be brooded over, to be ingested, to be lived with and *in*.

Eudora Welty is an imaginative writer. With her, nothing comes out of stock, and it has been impossible for her to stand still. Her art is a matter of contemplation, susceptibility, and discovery: it has been necessary for her to evolve for herself a language, and to arrive, each time she writes, at a new form. She has given us two collections of stories—*A Curtain of Green* and *The Wide Net*—a fairyless fairy tale called *The Robber Bridegroom,* and a novel, *Delta Wedding.* Now comes *The Golden Apples.*

The Golden Apples consists of seven stories similar in scene, playing upon the same cast of characters, dramatically different in time, and so placed in relation to one another as to develop a theme and bring out a pattern. The scene is the little town of Morgana, in the southern American state of Mississippi. The characters—whom we see in childhood, in adolescence, in maturity, in love, in death—are dwellers in and around Morgana. We more than see these people; we become identified with them, as though their

nerves, senses, and thoughts had been, by some opera-
tion, spliced into our own. The MacLains, the Starks,
the Spights, the Morrisons, the Raineys, and their
neighbours, each serve to illuminate for us intense
moments of experience, which are at once their own
and universal.

From whence has Miss Welty drawn her title? She
had in mind those golden apples which, rolled across
Atalanta's course as she ran, sent her chasing sideways, and made her lose the race. Outwardly, exist-
ences in Morgana—remote, sleepy, and past-bound
—are conventional: one goes to school, goes to work,
marries, raises one's family, dies. Inwardly, each of
these human beings gropes his or her way along—
perplexed, solitary (in spite of the neighbourliness),
and from time to time blinded by flashing illumina-
tions. We have the gentle albino, Snowdie MacLain,
and her almost magic relationship with her great,
handsome, errant husband. We have hoydenish
Virgie Rainey, with her abused music and her mis-
carried life. And young Loch Morrison, spying on
love and insanity in the deserted next-door house.
There are the MacLain twins (born of "the shower of
gold") and there is Jinny Love Stark, with her endless
girlhood enclosed in a gaunt marriage. Maideen,
wearer of dainty gloves, takes her own life after a
hallucinated episode of love. Cassie keeps her mother's name written in growing flowers. Old King
MacLain, all passion not quite spent, makes terrifying
grimaces at a funeral.

This is great, tender, austere stuff, shot through from beginning to end with beauty. Miss Welty does not merely decorate her style with similes and images, she uses them to enlarge it—such as here: *"Behind the bed the window was full of cloudy, pressing flowers and leaves in heavy light, like a jar of figs in syrup held up."* The seven episodes, or stories, in *The Golden Apples* are not to be separated from one another; they relate at once meaningly and closely: their dramatic total is only to be grasped at the very end—when time, with its action, and change, with its crushing force, seem, with Katie Rainey's burial, to reach full circle. So far as the stories *can* be made to stand apart, "The Shower of Gold," "June Recital," "Moon Lake," and "The Wanderers" are likely to be judged the most nearly perfect.

In *The Golden Apples*, Miss Welty would seem to have found, for her art, the ideal form. But, for a writer of her stature, nothing is conclusive—what comes next? American, deliberately regional in her settings, she "belongs," in the narrow sense, to no particular nation or continent, having found a communication which spans oceans.

—Books of Today

THE ECHOING GROVE *

THE PROBLEM of novel-writing is, how to convey. This may be forgotten, or overlooked, in days when

* *The Echoing Grove,* by Rosamond Lehmann. New York: Harcourt, Brace; 1953.

attention seems to be cast on the search for subject. A subject sufficiently unique, striking, should, some authors seem to consider, in itself be able to "carry" the book by its hold on the reader's startled imagination. Actually, what most often happens is that the book which depends on that kind of originality blazes a superficial course (that is, during the term of reading); but, when finished, dissipates in the mind. May it not be found that the classic, the majestic, the enduring novels treat of subjects which are rarely unique? The power is in the content; the authority is in the implied knowledge; the innovation is in the manner of telling. An elementary emotional situation, most often, provides the core. We may have ambition stories, life-stories, struggle-for-power stories; but the expectation that the novel should be a love story is hard to break down, and might not perhaps be broken down with impunity. Were it gone, fiction would fight a losing battle against documentary writing; the possibility of masterpieces would decline. The domain of the novel is, what continues to be irrational, yet inevitable, in human behaviour—hence, the novel's concern with the nature, and the effects, of love. We are shown not merely persons, but persons placed, willingly or otherwise, in each other's power.

The situation is timeless; yet, if it is to continue to be felt, it must be felt also, sharply, to be contemporary. Perhaps today, indeed, it seems all the odder —for today we attempt to clarify, we expect to plan, we suspect lesions, we denounce pressures. We have a strong, thinking addiction towards the social. Emotions are against the grain. This makes what might be called the persuasive telling of a love story (as apart from a sex story) much more difficult. This accentuates the novelist's main problem, of—as at first stated—how to convey. Rosamond Lehmann's handling of the problem is not the least of the triumphs of her novel *The Echoing Grove*. She has been so bold, in our time, as to picture the absoluteness, the entirety of love—its power to consume persons, and to consume itself. Her subject dominates, as the subject should—characters are taxed to the last inch, the time-continuity of the story is disrupted. Only consummate, considered, matured art on the part of a novelist could have achieved this—technical intricacy, sunk in the emotional power of the whole.

Scenes, incidents, radiate outward from the central factor—a man, Rickie, loved by his wife, Madeleine, has a love affair with Madeleine's sister, Dinah. The beginning of the story—in terms, that is, of Miss Lehmann's order of its narration—is in fact its end: the sisters, after fifteen years of estrangement, meet. Rickie is dead; years before his death there had been a break between him and Dinah, who has since then married, whose husband has been since then killed in the Spanish War. Madeleine is (on this late-autumn country afternoon when the widowed sisters go for a walk together) on the eve of a break with a

lover, Jocelyn, the beginning of her relationship
with whom had preceded Rickie's death. Rickie—
though this is known to neither sister—had, within
the last week of his life, become the lover of his
friend's wife, Georgie. Madeleine once, by an ill-
timed, well-meant call at her sister's flat, had inad-
vertently driven away the young man, Rob, with
whom Dinah was making a desperate experiment in
happiness. In the background had stood a refugee
doctor, Selby, with whom Dinah's relationship is
uncertain.

By being gradually given to know the whole, we
are caused cumulatively to feel it. When, with the last
pages of *The Echoing Grove,* we return to the sisters
alone together in the house by the river, in the autumn
night, we feel the ring-after-ring of significance round
each word which passes between them; we share
(with two dead men) knowledge of the origin of the
cigarette burn on the bedside table; we react to the
irony of the extreme lightness of a pair of cuff-links,
weighed on the palm of a woman's hand. What
seems the more remarkable is that at the outset—
when first we met these two women, as they meet on
the porch—we should have been caused by Miss
Lehmann to apprehend much that she had not even
begun to tell us. She charges herself with the relation
of incidents whose background cannot be estimated
till we have gathered (through travelling back in
time) what, and in what manner, had come before

them. It is extraordinary that we should be, from the first, so deeply implicated in what we do not yet even know that there is to know.

Much of the strength is due to the placing—that is, to the order of the scenes and their illuminating relation to one another. Each scene is, in effect, a dialogue —A with B, A with C, B with C, C with D, and so on. Seldom are more than two of the protagonists on the stage, or page, together. Unspoken soliloquies link, or frame, the dialogues. What might most nearly be confusing is the movement to and fro in time; the actual action, or, one might more fittingly say, activity, extends over more than ten years. There is not, however, confusion; thanks, in a great part, to Miss Lehmann's unfailing grip on her own time-scheme, and her carefulness in making it clear to us. By a series of light, sure touches—hints, reminders, clues—she instigates or refreshes the reader's memory. She justifies her reliance on concrete detail —the jade links, the Berlin woolwork armchair, glazed flower-pots, a pound note, a blue cotton frock, a pink evening gown.

The novel is well named. More than one of the characters is aware of love's claustrophobia; and indeed we stand with them in a shaded place in which voices are multiplied, sometimes mocked, by their own echoes, or by echoes of others. The book, in spite of its length and fullness, is constructed with a most masterful economy, in itself tense. Rickie, Dinah, Madeleine, unfold, deepen, gain in living complexity with the addition of each revealing scene. They fail one another; they diminish before each other's eyes. What is wrong—or is something in Nature changing? Change in women as women, in men as men, in their needs, in their efficacy for one another, is the suggested answer—even, the submerged theme. We are brought face to face with the tragic contemporary predicament: Modern Love.

—The New Republic

ALEXANDRIA *

To CAPTURE a city in writing is not easy; to encompass it, one must know where to begin. By consent, the more ancient the city, the more complex—yet the spectacular modern may give off in its own way something mixed and intense: there can be more atmosphere to a city than age accounts for. Further, some aged cities have a deceptive trick of throwing centuries off and, in some lights, looking new-built and raw. Apart from those which dissimulate, there are cities whose core of mystery dodges the seeking eye. On the whole, cities' personalities are evasive; one rates them the more highly for that reason. The officially "ancient" are the most docile—*there* remain some few monuments, which, in their isolation, at once speak for and simplify the enormous past.

It is not so in Alexandria. Alexandria sends the sightseer home hungry—sites are to be determined

* *Alexandria,* by E. M. Forster. New York: Anchor Books, Doubleday & Company; 1961.

by the lover or zealot, but little more. Two intersecting streets, still of importance, follow the courses of two wide main thoroughfares which, in their day, were columned from end to end—the marble's whiteness used to glare after dark. Otherwise there has been an obliteration of the original Greco-Egyptian grid plan. The Alexandria that was has been built over, incoherently, crowdedly, and loudly, by the Alexandria that has come to be. Visually, the first, renowned Alexandria leaves not a rack behind.

This was more than a city; it was a city-state, with the Greek as its prototype—accordingly, in itself a civilization. Unlike Athens or Rome, Alexandria never knew, or grew out of, primitive infancy. It was commanded into existence—immediate, adult, and dazzling—by Alexander the Great, who, having issued the order, went on, hot as ever for conquests and short of time. It seems he then completely forgot it. This, his "capital" on which he never set eyes, later received and entombed the prodigy's body. Around the mausoleum, the city obediently flowered out into what he had wished—before, that was, he had abandoned the Greek dream (as he so rapidly did) for the Oriental. But Alexandria, at the then mouth of the Nile, seat of the Ptolemies, came to be more than a memorial to Greece; it was itself a being, with generic visions and fevers. There was something belated and autumnal about its flowering, to be cut across by the first, somewhat gaunt springtide of Christian faith. Here was unpriceable wealth, the world's greatest library, then or now—to be sacked and burned in mob ecstasy, headed by purging monks. Till the saints marched in, the cosmopolitan city had magnetized scholars, nurtured philosophers, bred poets. Fitly, here, out of virulent controversy, was forged a creed, a hard-edged dogma, a logic. This was the intellectual birthplace of Christianity.

Alexandria seems to have made for drama, or been made for it—not amphitheatre drama but real life. Here, for instance, reigned Cleopatra. The climate, psychic or actual, perhaps enlarged or electrified personalities? The city's strategic value as a key port made it a prize in all Mediterranean strife for power. Rome annexed it, and after Rome came the Arabs. French or Turkish ambition and British interference raged around it in almost unceasing play. It is now Egypt's. What adds pungency to its history is that through all runs a continuous vein of irony.

Alexandrian Alexandria, together with its world-wonder Pharos, accustomed to sweep the dark with symbolic ray, has vanished—so did Atlantis. In its place, a compost. This 2,250-year-old city, close-packed with races, rackets, and religions, seems to exclude ghosts. "So far as I know there is no monograph on Alexandria." Could one wonder? But the speaker was about to take up his pen.

The meeting between a writer and his subject, though inevitable, might also seem a matter of fortuity. It took the fortunes of war to bring E. M. Forster to Alexandria. The time was autumn of

1915. As a civilian who had volunteered for the Red
Cross, the novelist found himself "dressed as a sort of
officer," and in, moreover, a slightly heroic mood—
Turkish invasion threatened: one might find oneself
in the battle line. The threat passed, anticlimax set in.
Here, for three years, he stuck to routine duties, un-
heroically safe through no fault of his. But there was
compensation. In times off he shed his officer guise
and sought renewal in his surroundings. "And it was
thus that I apprehended the magic and the antiquity
and the complexity of the city, and determined to
write about her. A guidebook suggested itself. I have
always respected guidebooks—particularly the earlier
Baedekers and Murrays—and I tried to work in some
history as well."

As an undertaking, this sounds modest. The outcome has been a beautiful job—a job, I repeat with
awe, that is truly beautiful. Though the tone of
modesty, of self-deprecation almost, is never lost. The
narrative is direct, curt; the style is quick, light, concrete. There is occasional malice or a whimsical smile.

Alexandria is a slim volume. How, in so small a
space, has the writer accomplished what I said at the
outset to be so difficult—encompassed a city—and of
all cities, maddening Alexandria? By means of art,
plus a touch of sixth sense. "Art," though, is a fuzzy
term when used in the Forster ambiance of precise
vocabulary. Art, here, has within it experience, patience, and initiative.

For me, Mr. Forster comes near being the ideal

writer, for this reason: that he knows (or has taught himself) not only what to do, but when to do it, and how to. *Alexandria,* the construction of which was a severe test, is a triumph of ability. Unostentatiously, this is a work of learning—lucid, for example, in its analysis of philosophies and religions. In the History part, this most dramatic of novelists rejoiced in the characters he confronted. As for irony, to him that is the breath of life. The Guide shows his passion for exactitude, also his tender respect for the preposterous—never a sneer! We have, too, his love of color (marigolds, painted buildings, flamingos); and, in the coastal and desert passages, his not mere view but vision of any landscape. It was well, for the city and the writer, that Alexandria came thus to be re-created.

This is the third edition of *Alexandria,* although its first publication in the United States. Where necessary, the Guide half has been brought up to date. Reading, one must not ignore the writer's instructions—to go to and fro between Parts I and II. "The 'History,' " he points out, "is written in short sections, and at the end of each are references to the second part, the 'Guide.' *On these references the utility of the book depends,* so the reader is begged to take special note of them." Good: so I did. But also, and simultaneously, one may need to be darting from one to another of the excellent maps. Holding the book *Alexandria* in my left hand, I found that my right required six fingers.

—The Reporter

BROADCASTS

SHE

(In 1947, the BBC Third Programme invited a succession of novelists, of which I was one, to talk about the book, or books, which had most impressed and affected them in their early days. Graham Greene's choice was also "a Rider Haggard," but he was so kind as to settle for King Solomon's Mines, *leaving me* She.)

AT THE AGE of twelve I was finding the world too small: it appeared to me like a dull, trim back garden, in which only trivial games could be played. The thunder-clouds which were to burst in 1914 were, of course, mounting on the horizon—but unobserved by me. Hemmed in by what seemed to be too much safety, I felt bored and hampered—ungrateful, but there you are: I still can distinctly remember the

228

sensation. Worse still, I had exhausted the myths of childhood. Fairy stories I never had cared for much, but up to now I had revelled in the companionship of violent adventurous book children. Now, a pall had fallen on them and me. I began to feel it was time we were growing up. Growing up to what?

My ideas of growing up were ambiguous, and sought to have no relation with reality. It was not easy, even in my own thoughts, to pin down my wish for accession to full power—fuller power, really, than I could see at work anywhere round me in the normal scene. Education had, if anything, been discouraging, my own romantic approaches to any subject being rebuffed in favour of quibbling truths. I developed a sort of grudge against actuality. History, for instance, had looked promising; but I soon found it inferior to the historical novel. I sustained, at about this time, a reverse in the matter of my fine essay on the Civil War. I had written:

"Now the Roundheads hated the Cavaliers because the Cavaliers were better-looking than they were. . . ."

"Oh," *they* said, returning the essay, "oh, but you can't say that!"

"Why—who says I can't say what?"

"You can't say that because it is not the case. Nothing, alas," *they* said, with a maddening kindly smile, "is quite so simple."

It was "alas," indeed. Constitutionalism: its first breath blew cold. I wanted the primary motive and the primary colour. So I resigned from history and turned to geography; if there were not a better time there might be a better place? But with geography, also, something shrivelled and shrank: there was no undiscovered country, they told me, now. What a prospect: what an absence of prospect, rather! I was chiefly depressed at that time, I think, by what seemed the sheer uniformity of the human lot, by its feebleness, arising from some deficiency. . . .

It was at the height of this, my first winter of discontent, that I came on the novel *She,* by Rider Haggard. Everything, from the first glance, made this a book of promise, even its author's name. Rider Haggard . . . was this some kind of Erl-king or demon horseman—staring, awful, visionary, and pale? Counterbalancing this, where I was concerned —for I had not a totally Gothic taste—was the book's cover: a solid, homely, and edible pink-brown, suggesting cocoa or milk chocolate. (And, indeed, in time the narrator's style, with its blend of the jocular and the blood-curdling, was to have on me the effect of well-sugared cocoa laced with some raw and subtle intoxicant.) It was impossible not to keep looking ahead at the wash illustrations by Greiffenhagen: a lion and crocodile locked in a death-grip . . . a savage dance in the dark, lit by human torches . . . a veiled white form proceeding down endless caves . . . an extinct, deserted city under the moon. . . .

Whether *She*—which, I see, was written in 1886—

was in the first place intended for grown-up people, I don't know. It announces itself as "a novel of adventure." It is a story of passion, out-size, direct—ideally directed, it would appear, to the frustrated, non-moral, pre-adolescent child. It gains, rather than loses, from the young reader's indifference to sex. Its soaring unrealism, its very enormities and deformities as a love story, were for me, really, in my time, its attraction.

Horace Holly, forty, a Cambridge don, looks ferocious like a baboon, but is mild at heart. Holly's ward, Leo Vincey, has gold curls and looks like a Greek god. Leo's twenty-fifth birthday is to be marked by the ceremonial opening of a family casket: it is revealed that the Vinceys, good old stock, trace descent from one Kallikrates, a priest of Isis. This Kallikrates broke his vows to marry, fled to Egypt, was shipwrecked on the Libyan coast, encountered the white queen of a savage tribe, and was by her slain—having failed to return her love for the good reason that he was married already. The vindictive queen, it remained on record, had bathed in the Fire of Everlasting Life. We are off—in the turn of a page we are She-ward bound.

"How different" (says Holly, who tells the story) "is the scene whereof I have now to tell from that which has now been told! Gone are the quiet college rooms, gone the wind-swayed English elms, the cawing rooks and the familiar volumes on the shelves. And in their place there rises a vision of the great calm ocean gleaming in shaded silver lights beneath the beams of a full African moon. . . . Three miles or more to our starboard is a low dim line. It is the Eastern shore of Central Africa—a perilous coast. The night is quiet, so quiet that a faint booming sound rolls across the water to us from the distant land.

"The Arab at the tiller holds up his hand and says one word:—'*Simba* (lion)!'

"Then it comes again, a slow majestic sound that thrills us to the marrow—"

The overture. Merely lion, but the first premonition—from now on Holly and I are to feel the suction of an inexorable magnetic force. The shipwreck, the unnerving appearance of the Amahagger tribesmen dwelling in cave-tombs inside the mountains, hot-potting their captives and ruled by She-who-must-be-obeyed.

"*Imperial Kôr is fallen, fallen!*" This is the cry that haunts Horace Holly's sleep. For these marshes and mountain-encircled plains show traces of a vanished civilization—haughty and grandiose. In the rock-chambers honeycombing the mountains lie—still immaculate after six thousand years of death—white-skinned aristocrats. Mild necrophily does, in fact, pervade the pages of *She:* dead beauties set up romantic loves in the dark rude male breasts of the Amahagger; and She-who-must-be-obeyed shares a bedroom-tomb with the preserved corpse of her beloved, the Kallikrates whom she had slain in a fit of

pique. . . . But Kôr, Kôr, the enormous derelict
city, whose streets the Amahagger dare not tread, is,
ever, on the horizon. My impatience to visit it was
immense—and my travellers, by this time deeply
embroiled with "She," made, for my tastes, madden-
ingly slow going. However, here we were at last:

"I wish," gasps Holly, "it lay within the power of
my pen to give any idea of the grandeur of the sight
which met our view. There, all bathed in the red glow
of the setting sun, were miles upon miles of ruins—
columns, temples, shrines and palaces of kings. . . .
Straight before us stretched away what had evidently
been the main thoroughfare of the city, for it was very
wide and regular, wider than the Thames Embankment. . . . In the fading light we passed swiftly up
the main road, that, I believe I am right in saying, no
human foot had pressed for thousands of years. . . ."

My spine crept. And, still, the moon was to rise—
"Court upon court, space upon space of empty cham-
bers, that spoke more eloquently to the imagination
than any crowded street. It was a wonderful sight to
see the full moon looking down on the ruined fane of
Kôr. A wonderful thing to think for how many
thousands of years the dead orb above and the dead
city below had thus gazed upon one another. . . .
The white light fell, and minute by minute the slow
shadows crept across the grass-grown courts."

I saw Kôr before I saw London; I was a provincial
child. Inevitably, the Thames Embankment was a
disappointment, being far, far less wide than Horace

Holly had led me to expect. I was inclined to see London as Kôr with the roofs still on. The idea that life in any capital city must be ephemeral, and with a doom ahead, remained with me—a curious obsession for an Edwardian child. At the same time I found something reassuring and comforting in the idea that, whatever happened, buildings survived people. Long, even, before I had read *She,* I would run across any amount of fields to look at any ruin, even the ruin of a cottage. Yes, it seems funny now . . . *She,* the book, glutted my imagination with images and pictures of which I could not, it seemed, have enough.

Can it have been the *mise en scène,* rather than the story itself, that, where I was concerned, turned some inside key? No, there was more than that to it. The reincarnation theme, then?—for Leo Vincey, of course, turned out to be reborn Kallikrates, and the whirlwind passion of She-who-must-be-obeyed was, at the first glance at Leo, again unleashed. She took up with Leo exactly where she had left off with Kallikrates. No, it was not *that,* exactly, either. (For one thing, I saw little point in Leo; were I to wait for someone for more than two thousand years, it would not be a jocular athlete with gold curls.) It was the idea of obstination, triumphant obstination, which became so obsessing—want any one thing hard enough, long enough, and it must come your way. This did strike deep: it came up like a reinforcement, because in my day, my childhood, all polite education was against the will—which was something to be subdued, or put out of sight as though it did not exist. Up to now, I had always expected books to be on the side of politeness. *She* contained thoughts and sayings I never had seen in print, and certainly never had heard spoken. Horace Holly, good man, disapproved of "She"—but how she impressed him! Impressed him? She swept him off his feet. In a fit of what he has set down as "mad passion" he at one point proposed marriage. Her unsuitability to be a Cambridge don's wife did not have to appear: she was set on Leo. Marriage to Leo, and a return to England to take over the government of that country, was her programme. Says Leo: "But we have a queen already."

"It is naught, it is naught. She can be overthrown!"

This really does worry Holly, who "meditated deeply on the awful nature of the problem that now opened before us. What her powers were I knew, and I could not doubt that she would exercise them to the full. . . . Her proud, ambitious spirit would be certain to break loose and avenge itself for the long centuries of solitude. In the end, I had little doubt, she would assume absolute rule over the British dominions, and probably the whole world. . . .

Did *I* then, I must ask, myself aspire to "She's" role? I honestly cannot say so. "She" was *she*—the out-size absolute of the grown-up. The exaltation I wanted was to be had from the looking on. She had entered fire (the thing of which I was most frightened). She shocked me, as agreeably and profoundly

as she shocked Horace Holly. For me, she continued
to have no face—I saw her as I preferred her, veiled,
veiled; two eyes burning their way through the layers
of gauze. Horace Holly's chaste categoric descriptions
of anything further left me cold. The undulating form
(even her neck, he told me, undulated at times), the
scented raven hair, the rounded arm, the "tiny san-
dalled foot," she could—where I was concerned—
keep. Or Leo could have them. Enviable?—no, they
were mere accessories. She gave me ideas, yes—but
not all ideas: I was still twelve.

I read *She,* dreamed *She,* lived *She* for a year and a
half. . . . Since then, until almost yesterday, I have
not opened the chocolate-pink book again. There are
—there can but be—startling divagations between
what I remember and what is written. At the same
time, surprisingly little of what *was* written has evaporated. All the way there is an echo-track of sensation
—just as I find my own childish grubby thumb-prints
on the pages.

This book *She* is for me historic—it stands for the
first totally violent impact I ever received from print.
After *She,* print was to fill me with apprehension. I
was prepared to handle any book like a bomb. It was
—did I realize that all the time?—Horace Holly, not
ever, really, She-who-must-be-obeyed, who controlled
the magic. Writing—that creaking, pedantic, obtrusive, arch, prudish, opaque, over-worded *writing*
. . . what it could do! That was the revelation; that
was the power in the cave. The power whose in-

equality dear Holly laments at the opening of every passage. The power of the pen. The inventive pen.

TRUTH AND FICTION

(The following are three unscripted talks about the Novel, given on the BBC Home Service in the autumn of 1956. The talks were recorded as they were spoken; and in that form they are given here. Repetitions, overemphasis, incoherences, etc., must be allowed for.)

I

STORY

WHAT is a novel? I say: an invented story. At the same time a story which, though invented, has the power to ring true. True to what? True to life as the reader knows life to be or, it may be, feels life to be. And I mean the adult, the grown-up reader. Such a reader has outgrown fairy tales, and we do not want the fantastic and the impossible. So I say to you that a novel must stand up to the adult tests of reality.

You may say: "If one wants truth, why not go to the literally true book? Biography or documentary, these amazing accounts of amazing experiences which people have." Yes, but I am suggesting to you that there is a distinction between truth and so-called reality. What these people write in their accounts of happenings is actually and factually true, but the novel is not confining itself to what happened. The novel does not simply recount experience, it adds to experience. I hope you will see what I mean. It is not news at all, not anything sensational or spectacular. And here comes in what is the actual livening spark of the novel: the novelist's imagination has a power of its own. It does not merely invent, it perceives. It intensifies, therefore it gives power, extra importance, greater truth, and greater inner reality to what well may be ordinary and everyday things.

So much is art—the art that, in common with poetry, drama, painting, and music, does, we all know, enter into the novel. But not less and absolutely joined with the art is craft, and craft—craftsmanship —is absolutely and surely an essential for the writing of a novel. I have said the novel is story. It is the story aspect that I am talking about first and now, and the craft of the novelist does lie first of all in story-telling.

What is a good story? I give you three things which strike me. First, it is simple—by which I mean straightforward, easy to grasp, and therefore liable to be well remembered. Do you think by stressing simplicity I perhaps simplify too much? Do we say: "Ah, but what about such books as *The Brothers Karamazov;* would you call such a story simple?" No, I would not; it is full of halts and magnificent confusions—at least to me. And therefore by my definition I would call *The Brothers Karamazov* a great book, but not, in the craftsmanship sense, a good novel. Novelists out-and-out do recognize what is a good story. It is part of their craft to perceive what story is. Look how brilliant in their choices—in their finding of stories—have been Dickens, Jane Austen,

Balzac, Conrad, Hardy, Tolstoi, to name only a few of what we now call the classics. And, among contemporaries, is not the same true of Graham Greene, or E. M. Forster, Joyce Cary, Hemingway, and many others who pass with you and of whom you will probably think now?

The next mark of a good story is, surely, its general interest. The good story, to put it as shortly as I can, turns upon some crisis, or problem, which would be of importance, intense importance, to us; to you and me in our own lives.

Then the third essential of the good story—a good story takes off well. It takes off from a situation which holds promise, or at any rate it suggests that such a situation is to be. There I am generalizing. I do say to you that it is not fair to judge all novels, even the best, by their opening pages. But, speaking as a reader, I must say that I myself am tremendously influenced for or against a book by the manner of the opening, and that as a novelist myself I have put great stress and interest into the openings of my own books. And though they are open to every criticism, I still would stand by the first two pages of most of the novels I ever wrote. However, to get to something more interesting and further from me, here are three examples of openings; and I want you to notice that in each we get the seed of the character of the whole book from this first initial scene.

While the present century was in its teens, and on one sunshiny morning in June, there drove up to the great iron gate of Miss Pinkerton's academy for young ladies, on Chiswick Mall, a large family coach, with two fat horses in blazing harness, driven by a fat coachman in a three-cornered hat and wig, at the rate of four miles an hour. A black servant, who reposed on the box beside the fat coachman, uncurled his bandy legs as soon as the equipage drew up opposite Miss Pinkerton's shining brass plate, and as he pulled the bell, at least a score of young heads were seen peering out of the narrow windows of the stately old brick house. Nay, the acute observer might have recognised the little red nose of good-natured Miss Jemima Pinkerton herself, rising over some geranium-pots in the window of that lady's own drawing-room.

"It is Mrs. Sedley's coach, sister," said Miss Jemima. "Sambo, the black servant, has just rung the bell; and the coachman has a new red waistcoat."

"Have you completed all the necessary preparations incident to Miss Sedley's departure, Miss Jemima?" asked Miss Pinkerton herself, that majestic lady; the Semiramis of Hammersmith, the friend of Doctor Johnson, the correspondent of Mrs. Chapone herself.

"The girls were up at four this morning, packing her trunks, sister," replied Miss Jemima; "we have made her a bow-pot."

"Say a bouquet, sister Jemima, 'tis more genteel."

"Well, a booky as big almost as a hay-stack! I have put up two bottles of the gillyflower-water for Mrs. Sedley, and the receipt for making it, in Amelia's box."

"And I trust, Miss Jemima, you have made a copy of Miss Sedley's account. This is it, is it? Very good—ninety-three pounds, four shillings."

You will know that, I expect? The first page of *Vanity Fair*. What writing for the eye, isn't it? Doesn't that strike you? One is reminded that

Thackeray was also a first-rate comic draughtsman, and do you notice how he whisks us from the outside into the inside of the house? Also what a foretaste: we know the note of the book. It is to be satire, you can see all those small, deft satirical flicks —the theme is going to be worldliness, success-mania and all its attendant absurdities. It is also magnificent stage-setting; the stage is set. For whom? Who is to enter? Becky Sharp. I give you *Vanity Fair* as an extreme satiric example of one whole big group of fiction, the social novel.

Here is something totally different:

Hale knew, before he had been in Brighton three hours, that they meant to murder him. With his inky fingers and his bitten nails, his manner cynical and nervous, anybody could tell he didn't belong—belong to the early summer sun, the cool Whitsun wind off the sea, the holiday crowd. They came in by train from Victoria every five minutes, rocked down Queen's Road standing on the tops of the little local trams, stepped off in bewildered multitudes into fresh and glittering air: the new silver paint sparkled on the piers, the cream houses ran away into the west like a pale Victorian water-colour; a race in miniature motors, a band playing, flower gardens in bloom below the front, an aeroplane advertising something for the health in pale vanishing clouds across the sky.

It had seemed quite easy to Hale to be lost in Brighton. Fifty thousand people besides himself were down for the day, and for quite a while he gave himself up to the good day, drinking gins and tonics whenever his programme allowed. For he had to stick closely to a programme: from ten till eleven Queen's Road and Castle Square, from eleven till twelve the Aquarium and Palace Pier, twelve till one the front between the Old Ship and West Pier, back for lunch between one and two in any restaurant he chose round the Castle Square, and after that he had to make his way all down the parade to the West Pier and then to the station by the Hove streets. These were the limits of his absurd and widely advertised sentry go.

The first page of Graham Greene's *Brighton Rock:* straight off, we go into danger; the undertow of suspense and fear—the thing isolating one man from fifty thousand. Again wonderful scene-setting. You will have reacted to the immense contrast between the scene and the man; the irony of the band playing, the bright glistening paint, the Whitsun sunshine. This could be the opening of a first-rate thriller—and why not? Graham Greene's genius is contemporary; he is master of the technique which is in essence twentieth century. Tautness, quickness, and what Sartre has called the "extreme situation." There is something in that technique in common with the cinema; something, yes, in common with the thriller; swift-moving and for the eye; dry, anti-emotional. Yes, but there is more to this. Graham Greene is using all this quick technique, this sense of imminent danger, for a purpose of his own. He deals in danger, yes; but the danger is more than danger to the flesh— it is danger to the soul. So the crisis is internal. And Graham Greene's novels head what is now a prominent group of fiction—the novel of action—though

242

indeed he would not be what he is if he dealt only with action in the outward, physical sense.

Now I want an opening in another period of time:

There was no possibility of taking a walk that day. We had been wandering, indeed, in the leafless shrubbery an hour in the morning; but since dinner (Mrs. Reed, when there was no company, dined early) the cold winter wind had brought with it clouds so sombre, and a rain so penetrating, that further out-door exercise was now out of the question.

I was glad of it: I never liked long walks, especially on chilly afternoons: dreadful to me was the coming home in the raw twilight, with nipped fingers and toes, and a heart saddened by the chidings of Bessie, the nurse, and humbled by the consciousness of my physical inferiority to Eliza, John, and Georgiana Reed.

The said Eliza, John, and Georgiana were now clustered round their mama in the drawing-room: she lay reclined on a sofa by the fireside, and with her darlings about her (for the time neither quarrelling nor crying) looked perfectly happy. Me, she had dispensed from joining the group; saying, "She regretted to be under the necessity of keeping me at a distance; but that until she heard from Bessie, and could discover by her own observation that I was endeavouring in good earnest to acquire a more sociable and childlike disposition, a more attractive and sprightly manner—something lighter, franker, more natural as it were—she really must exclude me from privileges intended only for contented, happy, little children."

"What does Bessie say I have done?" I asked.

Charlotte Brontë's opening into *Jane Eyre*. The keynote—immediate—and in how few words! We see the child Jane as life has already made her—solitary, sombre, isolated, unyielding. Exclusion seems to be her fate. But she does not sit down, you will notice, under injustice. Boldly she asks that point-blank question: "What does Bessie say I have done?" This is to be the Jane of the after years; alone against the world and yet always flying her own flag.

Charlotte Brontë, like Graham Greene, has used contrast to build up immediate drama. The excluded child on a bitterly cold day against the cosy, glowing family group in the firelight. This exile from happiness is to repeat and repeat itself throughout the novel. *Jane Eyre* is one of the most outstanding of a third group again, the character novel, and that is not simply a novel in which character plays a great part —because character does that in all novels—but one in which the story is architected round a single person, and one in which, usually, such persons show power to influence their own destiny so that the story springs from them. Things happen because of what they are and what they do. In themselves they precipitate situations. You will think of innumerable other examples of the character novel, *David Copperfield*, *Madame Bovary*, *Tom Jones*.

It seems to me today that we have fewer character novels. Is that because, do you think, we are less now concerned with individuals' destiny, or is it because the social novel with the questions it brings up, or the action novel with its clear-cut issues, appeals more to our kind of imagination?

244

There is a tremendous further thing in the story. I do not mean by "story" simply the "plot"—the outline of the happenings. There must be story in that sense: cause and effect, the keeping of suspense in play; the "What next?" element. But something else is necessary to the story if the novel is to have the proportions it should have. We need a theme—an inner subject. The theme is what the novel is about, and, still more, it is the reason for the novel. You may know how difficult it is, if you are impressed by a book you are reading, and somebody says: "What is it about?" You outline the superficial plot or story and your friend may say: "Well, I've heard of all that before." And really in order to convey the effect that the novel is having on you, you would have to plunge a degree more deeply and find words, if you could, if you had time, for the underlying idea which gives the reason why the story should be told, and the reason why the story is important and hits you.

I think that in almost all cases the theme, or the idea, of the novel has come first of all to the mind of the author, and he has shaped his plot in order to express it and conceived of his characters in terms of it. It is the kindling spark—the ignition spark—that is in his mind when he says: "I've got an idea for a story!"

Let us consider some themes: *Vanity Fair* we have touched on—worldliness, its absurdities. Of *Brighton Rock,* one would say guilt and the danger which it involves. Other themes: conscience in Trollope's *The*

245

Warden, and recently, in a novel of this year, Angus Wilson's *Anglo-Saxon Attitudes.* Love of power: *Emma, Barchester Towers;* and, in France, in many of the Balzac stories; in contemporary Britain in almost all of the Ivy Compton-Burnett novels. Self-deception: *Great Expectations,* and, again, *Emma.* (Often a novel may have a dual theme.) Self-redemption: *Lord Jim; The Power and the Glory.* Frustration: *Jude the Obscure.* Real versus unreal values: *Howards End,* and, indeed, I think all the E. M. Forster novels.

Two attributes the theme must have: the moral element, because it is through the theme that the novelist makes his evaluations or shows some new aspect of truth which has struck him: and again the theme must be deeply submerged in the story. If a theme or idea is too near the surface, the novel becomes simply a tract illustrating an idea. I do not mean theme in that way. It is something of which you will feel the effects and which works strongly for the novelist but which is down so deep that you may have to analyze the story to find what it actually is.

Besides theme, the story must have another thing: situation. The situation is something more than a series of episodes and happenings through which the story moves. There is nearly always an over-all situation which is a "controlling" thing. Often it is a situation between two persons: the unhappy passion of Anna and Vronsky in *Anna Karenina,* or in *Wuther-*

ing Heights the stronger-than-death tie between Catherine and Heathcliff. There are endless variants of this situation between two persons which maintains through a book. For instance, enslavement—or disillusionment. But the situation can also be a circumstance. It can be the situation of somebody being extremely poor and being thrust into some kind of behaviour because of it. It can be a craving for education as in *Jude the Obscure,* or the idealization of a great house and family as in Evelyn Waugh's *Brideshead Revisited.* And throughout Proust's long masterpiece there is his absorption in his own romantic conceptions of person after person who comes his way. I would call that situation.

I have said only exceedingly few of the things which could be said about the aspect of the novel as story. I have said that though the story is invented it must ring true through the power of imagination, which is something higher than invention. It has a form of vision which makes for a peculiar truth. I have said that not only art but craftsmanship is necessary for the bringing alive of story, and that the story, besides its plot—however well built and exciting— must have an internal theme, and must hinge round some over-all situation which must clearly be an interesting one. It is the presence of theme above all which demarcates the novel, and the greater the theme and the more imaginatively it is worked out, the greater the novel.

There are excellent forms of story, like the detective story or thriller, which do not claim to have theme. We react to and we enjoy the sheer suspense element and the quick action. But I think the failure of theme—the failure of a really important inside idea—shows in the kind of novel which is inferior. It is hard to say why: the story may be good, the characters may be amusingly touched in, but if at the end of a novel we put it down and it evaporates from our minds—if then we care to go back and see why that book has seemed less important and not worth more than the few hours for which it entertained us—we will almost always find that the novelist has not had either a conception or a grasp of some inner, underlying important idea. And those ideas can be worked out perfectly well in comedy and satire. I do not want to leave in your minds the idea that a novel must be pompous or didactic.

Finally, you may say: "Do you confine the novel to something which has an evident outward story?" And you will bring up some of the most interesting experiments of this century in which we live, the works, say, of Kafka or of James Joyce. I say that there is always story in a novel, but it may be on some different and unexpected plane: it may be psychological, emotional, or internal. And I cannot think of a better example of psychological story than the culminating masterpiece of James Joyce—*Ulysses*. It moves forward: it moves throughout a day—and the test of a story is that it does move forward.

II

PEOPLE

WOULD you or I, as readers, be drawn into a novel—
implicated with what may be its other issues—at all,
if our interest was not pegged to the personalities and
the outlooks and the actions of the people whom we
encounter inside the story? They are the attractive
element in the book.

This being so, which comes first actually into the
mind of the novelist when he begins to work: the
people (or characters) or the plot? Do not think it
strange when I say that the plot comes first. The
actual idea or outline of a book is there—the possibilities of a situation—and then the novelist thinks:
"What would be the kind of person who would perform such an action? What would be the other kind of
person who would react in a particular way?" I think
to myself: "I need a proud man," or "I need a woman
so idiotically romantic in temperament that she will
do unwise things," or "I need perhaps an almost
excessively innocent or ignorant young person." In
that sense the characters are called into existence by
the demands of the plot; but I do not want you to
feel that the characters are merely invented to formula. That is not so at all. Their existence having
begun, they take into themselves a most extraordinary
and imperative reality. And their relation with plot is
a dual one because, though to an extent the demands
of the plot control them, the plot also serves to give

them force and purpose. And, because of the plot, those characters are so shown and so brought into action that as little as possible of them shall go to waste.

The people, the characters in a novel, must carry with them into the book their own kind of inevitability. We are conscious when we meet the people involved in a story that they have something within them which will probably take them towards some inevitable fate or end. If that inevitability breaks down—if the characters are compelled by the author to do what we instinctively know they would not do—then I think we feel that there is a flaw in the reality of the novel.

How does the novelist bring his people in? A great question—and it comes early on—is the showing, or the presentation, of the characters. We want to see them, we want to feel them, and we want to have some idea of what they are about, as it were, in the story, and what kind of part it is highly probably that they will play. I want to give you an example first from the early Henry James, from the novel *Portrait of a Lady*. Visualize the scene: it is a summer day in the evening, and on the lawn of an English country house by the Thames two gentlemen are strolling in conversation.

One of these was a remarkably well-made man of five-and-thirty, with a face as English as that of the old gentle-man I have just sketched was something else; a noticeably handsome face, fresh-coloured, fair and frank, with firm,

straight features, a lively grey eye and the rich adornment
of a chestnut beard. This person had a certain fortunate,
brilliant, exceptional look—the air of a happy temperament fertilised by a high civilisation—which would have
made almost any observer envy him at a venture. He was
booted and spurred, as if he had dismounted from a long
ride; he wore a white hat, which looked too large for him;
he held his two hands behind him, and in one of them—a
large, white, well-shaped fist—was crumpled a pair of
soiled dog-skin gloves.

His companion, measuring the length of the lawn beside
him, was a person of quite a different pattern, who, although he might have excited grave curiosity, would not,
like the other, have provoked you to wish yourself, almost
blindly, in his place. Tall, lean, loosely and feebly put
together, he had an ugly, sickly, witty, charming face,
furnished, but by no means decorated, with a straggling
moustache and whisker. He looked clever and ill—a
combination by no means felicitous; and he wore a brown
velvet jacket. He carried his hands in his pockets, and
there was something in the way he did it that showed the
habit was inveterate. His gait had a shambling, wandering
quality; he was not very firm on his legs.

The first of those is a young English lord; the
second is a highly intelligent American expatriate—
something perhaps in common with Henry James and
the type with whom he dealt so much. You will see
how those small descriptive touches are none of them
put in in a purely categorical way, and how the first
young man is saved from being aggressively successful, aggressively privileged, by those odd little touches
of eccentricity. His hat is too big, his crumpled gloves

are rather soiled. And the second, there is something straggling—straggling in the moustache, straggling in the way he walks about—and yet we feel in that second man this sensitive, complex, deeply responsive strain. Neither of these two men is the central character. Isabel Archer is in a moment more to walk through the door of the house and across the lawn to meet them. These two characters are to play a tremendous part in her life, and I think the kind of role which each will play in their love for her and their desire to help her is indicated in those two very short paragraphs in which Henry James has first shown them to us.

But there is not only the question of showing, of presenting, of introducing the characters. There is the still—I think—trickier one of keeping them in play, perpetually in the view of the reader, engaged in the action and also furthering the development of the plot. And this is done in two ways; either by analysis or by dialogue. Analysis has always been used. It was the original loose, comfortable, descriptive method which the late eighteenth-century people and the Victorians employed. The writer stepped in, he intervened, he explained the actions of his characters, and he himself described their thoughts or emotions. But the other, the more recent and the more subtle kind of character analysis, which I think is most peculiar to the early part of the twentieth century, was called the "stream of consciousness," and that had as its exponents such people as Dorothy Richardson,

George Meredith, Proust, Henry James (increasingly as his work went on), James Joyce, and sometimes, though not to so great an extent, Virginia Woolf. This showed characters, not through explanations, but through the thoughts which occurred to them and the sensations which they had. Consider this from Dorothy Richardson, out of one of the novels in the Miriam sequence which is called *The Tunnel*.

At Gower Street it was eleven o'clock. She was faint with hunger. She had had no dinner and there was nothing in her room. She wandered along the Euston Road hoping to meet a potato-man. The shop fronts were black. There was nothing to meet her need but the empty stretch of lamplit pavement leading on and on. Rapid walking in the rain-freshened air relieved her faintness, but she dreaded waking in the night with gnawing hunger to keep her awake and drag her up exhausted in the morning. A faint square of brighter light on the pavement ahead came like an accusation. Passing swiftly across it she glanced bitterly at the frosted door through which it came. Restaurant. Donizetti Brothers. The whole world had conspired to leave her alone with that mystery, shut in and hidden every day the whole of her London time behind its closed frosted front doors and forcing her now to admit that there was food there and that she must go in or have the knowledge of being starved through fear. Her thoughts flashed painfully across a frosted door long ago in Baker Street, and she saw the angry handsome face of the waiter who had shouted "Roll and butter" and whisked away from the table the twisted cone of serviette and the knives and forks. That was the middle of the day. It would be worse at night. Perhaps they would even refuse to serve her. Perhaps it was impossible to go into a restaurant late at night alone. She was coming back. There was nothing to be seen behind the steamy panes on either side of the door but plants standing on oil-cloth mats. Behind them was again frosted glass. It was not so grand as Baker Street. There was no menu in a large glass frame with "Schweppe's" at the top. She pushed open the glass door and was confronted by another glass door blankly frosted all over. Why were they so secret?

You see how that works. Outwardly we have a street and the entrance to the restaurant, but all of it is photographed in terms of subjectivity of a hungry, tired, and, above all, nervous and dread-filled young woman who is trying to make up her mind to go in and buy herself a meal. Why does the light show like an accusation? Because here is something that she must face—food; but has she got the nerve to go in and order her small cheap meal? . . . And the idea of secrecy and the restaurant being kept back as a sort of conspiratorial mystery. Here is somebody alone in London, and the entire five books of the sequence are devoted to this extraordinary reaction of one personality to what are outwardly perfectly ordinary circumstances to the Londoner who takes them for granted.

Two things may be remarked about the "stream of consciousness" in the showing of character. It does take time and it deals almost always with prosaic experience seen or reacted to in a highly individual way. I do not know whether we should ever have, for instance, a stream-of-consciousness novel about somebody scaling Everest, because the scaling of Everest is exciting enough in itself. In the ordinary "stream of consciousness," the excitement, the sense of crisis, resides in the personality, and all the other characters in the novel are likely to be slightly out of focus.

I want tremendously to go straight on to the question of the dialogue. Dialogue is much more the *contemporary* way of keeping in evidence—keeping in play—the characters in a book, and I think a satisfactory reason for this is that it is arresting and entertaining and clear-cut and highly personal. Jane Austen, much in advance of her day, was a mistress of the use of the dialogue. She used it as dialogue should be used —to advance the story; not only to show the characters but to advance. Here, in this extract from *Mansfield Park,* you will find three characters—Fanny, the little poor relation; Lady Bertram, the overpowering and rather selfish aunt who is not only Fanny's relation but her employer; and Edmund, the son of Lady Bertram —all confronted by a situation which has never come up before. Fanny, mouse, accustomed to being ignored, has for the first time been invited to a formal dinner party.

"But why should Mrs. Grant ask Fanny?" said Lady Bertram. "How came she to think of asking Fanny?— Fanny never dines there, you know, in this sort of way. I cannot spare her, and I am sure she does not want to go.— Fanny, you do not want to go, do you?"

"If you put such a question to her," cried Edmund, preventing his cousin's speaking, "Fanny will immediately say, no; but I am sure, my dear mother, she would like to go; and I can see no reason why she should not."

"I cannot imagine why Mrs. Grant should think of asking her?—She never did before.—She used to ask your sisters now and then, but she never asked Fanny."

"If you cannot do without me, ma'am," said Fanny, in a self-denying tone—

"But my mother will have my father with her all the evening."

"To be sure, so I shall."

"Suppose you take my father's opinion, ma'am."

"That's well thought of. So I will, Edmund. I will ask Sir Thomas, as soon as he comes in, whether I can do without her."

"As you please, ma'am, on that head; but I meant my father's opinion as to the *propriety* of the invitation's being accepted or not; and I think he will consider it a right thing by Mrs. Grant, as well as by Fanny, that being the *first* invitation it should be accepted."

"I do not know. We will ask him. But he will be very much surprised that Mrs. Grant should ask Fanny at all."

We learn something, as I said, of the relationships between these three, brought out by the small social crisis. We are in the grip of something which, in this undisturbed world of the big, bland country house, Mansfield Park, has not happened before. All good dialogue perhaps deals with something unprecedented. Here now is a totally different manner. It is a piece from E. M. Forster's *Howards End*. The circumstances are that Margaret Schlegel, recently engaged to the widower Henry Wilcox, is on her way to the wedding of Henry's daughter, which is to take place in a house in Shropshire. She is in company with a number of other people, all of whom are the friends of the Wilcoxes, belonging to what might be described as their gang.

"That was the Grange," remarked Albert, over his shoulder, and then he jammed the brake on, and the motor slowed down and stopped. "I'm sorry," said he turning round. "Do you mind getting out—by the door, on the right. Steady on."

"What's happened?" asked Mrs. Warrington.

Then the car behind them drew up and the voice of Charles was heard saying: "Get out the women at once." There was a concourse of males, and Margaret and her companions were hustled out and received into the second car. What had happened? As it started off again the door of a cottage opened, and a girl screamed wildly at them.

"What is it?" the ladies cried.

Charles drove them a hundred yards without speaking. Then he said: "It's all right. Your car just touched a dog."

"But stop!" cried Margaret, horrified.

"It didn't hurt him."

"Didn't really hurt him?" asked Myra.

"No."

"Do *please* stop!" said Margaret, leaning forward. She was standing up in the car, the other occupants holding her knees to steady her. "I want to go back, please."

Charles took no notice.

"We've left Mr. Fussell behind," said another: "and Angelo, and Crane."

"Yes, but no woman."

"I expect a little of"—Mrs. Warrington scratched her palm—"will be more to the point than one of us!"

"The insurance company sees to that," remarked Charles, "and Albert will do the talking."

"I want to go back, though, I say!" repeated Margaret, getting angry.

Charles took no notice. The motor, loaded with refugees, continued to travel very slowly down the hill. "The men are there," chorused the others. "Men will see to it."

"The men *can't* see to it. Oh, this is ridiculous! Charles, I ask you to stop."

"Stopping's no good," drawled Charles.

"Isn't it?" said Margaret, and jumped straight out of the car.

She fell on her knees, cut her gloves, shook her hat over her ear. Cries of alarm followed her. "You've hurt yourself!" exclaimed Charles, jumping after her.

"Of course I've hurt myself!" she retorted.

"May I ask what—"

"There's nothing to ask," said Margaret.

"Your hand's bleeding."

"I know."

"I'm in for a frightful row from the pater."

"You should have thought of that sooner, Charles."

Charles had never been in such a position before. It was a woman in revolt who was hobbling away from him, and the sight was too strange to leave any room for anger. He recovered himself when the others caught them up: their sort he understood. He commanded them to go back.

Albert Fussell was seen walking towards them.

"It's all right!" he called. "It wasn't a dog, it was a cat."

"There!" exclaimed Charles triumphantly. "It's only a rotten cat."

You might call that a fight more than a conversation. The Schlegel-Wilcox antagonism has flared up and all because of "a rotten cat." Can Margaret Schlegel marry into this family, have this awful

Charles as a stepson? *Howards End,* for all its Edwardian surface, is a violent novel. It contains five, six, seven really explosive scenes. It is pitched high. What causes this protracted crisis? Conflicting values, opposing views of life. And such a novel, with such a theme of conflict, could not, I am sure, have been written analytically. It is essential for the author's purpose to keep the characters human, spontaneous, and naturalistic. They must be close up to the eye, close to one's feelings the whole time, otherwise *Howards End* could have been an abstract tract.

Both these authors, Jane Austen and E. M. Forster, have come into a renewed kind of prominence since the value of dialogue has been realized, and since we turn more and more to the dialogue-telling of the story. There have been changes in the use and the conception of dialogue. About thirty years ago the prevailing mode of expression was the analytical, which perhaps was a little misty and a little slow, and through this kind of smoke-screen of continuous analysis broke out, not long after the First World War, this sharp, clear-cut, almost rowdy dialogue of which the younger Hemingway was the great exponent.

But is there not now an emergence of dialogue of a different kind—stylized, formalized? I call your attention to the use of dialogue in two of our immediately contemporary authors—Henry Green and Ivy Compton-Burnett. In these we have a dialogue which is not representative of the person, which does not aim

in its own way to sound either realistic or spontaneous.
Here is an extract from Miss Compton-Burnett's novel
Elders and Betters:

Thomas had heard his children in silence.
"Ought you not to be teaching Reuben, my boy?"
"I am teaching him, Father."
"And how are you contriving that?"
"By my own odd methods, that will have a better
result than ordinary ones. Or that is the kind of thing that
would happen."
"He is doing something for you, I suppose?"
"He is learning to use his brain for himself, which is
the end of all education."
"But is it the beginning?"
"The same thing is always both. The beginning and the
end, we say. I never quite understand it."
"I suppose you will go and point out his mistakes?"
"I shall let him see them for himself."
"But if he could do that, he would hardly make them."
"You must know that we learn by our mistakes,
Father."
"Has he any need of you?"
"Great need, the poor, untaught lad."
"What does he think of your methods?"
"He does not think; that is not a thing he would do.
He is gaining self-respect from them. And he will gain
independence; and that is what I want, or I should have
to spend my time with him."
"What is his feeling for you?"
"A boyish veneration that will soon approach worship.
I shall not feel so free when it reaches that. I shall find
it has acquired its own value."
"What would Anna say to your methods?"

"She would think that Uncle Benjamin ought not to pay me."

"And do you think he ought?" said Thomas.

"Well, my service is of a kind that cannot be paid for in money. And that means it is paid for in that way, but not very well."

"Does your uncle want that kind of service?"

"Yes, or he would have to pay better."

"He has a larger income than we have," said Tullia. "And yet they are to spend their lives in that awkward house."

No: decidedly *not* a form of character portraiture. All the characters in a Compton-Burnett novel speak, as you will know, more or less alike—young and old, powerful and humble. Dialogue is used, as in a parallel way Henry Green does use it, apparently as an end in itself. And yet nothing in the novel is an end in itself. The novel is the end and aim of the author. Are we to take it—I leave you, in closing, with this suggestion—that this change in the manner and use of a dialogue denotes or symbolizes some change in the form of the novel, and still more in the intentions of the novel in our day? Does it mark the ending of a study of individualized character, the individual for his own sake, as a theme? Are we going back to the symbolic, the masked speaker? Is this turning away from naturalism a lapse or suspension of interest in single people and a greater sense, on our part, of the importance of crisis or the meaning of group emotion and group feeling? Do we think more of *kinds* of people?

One thing we may be certain of—people are the novel's concern, and with people the novel will remain involved; though who they are and what parts they are to play may change with time and the showing may change accordingly.

I I I

TIME

TIME is a major component of the novel. I rate it at the same value as story and character. I can think of few novelists who really know, and instinctively know, their craft who do not put time to dramatic use. Let us look at some of the ways in which this is done.

First, there are books in which time may rank almost among the characters and be even the chief character. What an example is *War and Peace!* In this, time acts on people; they react to it. We watch a large number of characters confronting each other in the presence of changing time and in the grip of the dramas and the solutions which time produces. Because of this, it is totally different from some imaginary, pleasant, topical, chatty little novel that we might have had some years ago, called *The Joneses in War and Peace,* which would have been a superficial view of people reacting to violent circumstances.

Another use for time is that it plays a great part in suspense: the "What next?" which in a story is so essential. In the good thriller you hear almost the time-bomb-like ticking of a clock, but also in what we may call the serious novel we are, or should be, conscious of a clock that strikes from hour to hour and the leaves of a calendar which turn over. Again, time pins the reader to that immense "Now" which is so important if we are to have a feeling of concern and reality with the novel. The good story is a succession of effective Nows—call them scenes, if you like—and those Nows are linked together by intermediate action. We may move backwards and forwards, but the present moment must grip and hold us, so that while we read it is as important, more important than the moment in the room where we are in our chair.

I think myself that a master of the dramatic Now was Virginia Woolf, and I want to give you an instance of her use of that extraordinary simultaneousness in which a number of things may be made dramatic by happening close to each other. Here is an extract from *Mrs. Dalloway*. The scene is Bond Street, London, on a June morning. Everything is at its height, a car has stopped unaccountably outside the windows of a flower-shop.

—oh! a pistol shot in the street outside!

"Dear, those motor cars," said Miss Pym, going to the window to look, and coming back and smiling apologetically with her hands full of sweet peas, as if those motor cars, those tyres of motor cars, were all *her* fault.

The violent explosion which made Mrs. Dalloway jump and Miss Pym go to the window and apologise came from a motor car which had drawn to the side of the pavement precisely opposite Mulberry's shop window. Passers-by who, of course, stopped and stared, had just time to see a face of the very greatest importance against the dove-grey upholstery, before a male hand drew the blind and there was nothing to be seen except a square of dove grey.

Yet rumors were at once in circulation from the middle of Bond Street to Oxford Street on one side, to Atkinson's scent shop on the other, passing invisibly, inaudibly, like a cloud, swift, veil-like upon hills, falling indeed with something of a cloud's sudden sobriety and stillness upon faces which a second before had been utterly disorderly. But now mystery had brushed them with her wing; they had heard the voice of authority; the spirit of religion was abroad with her eyes bandaged tight and her lips gaping wide. But nobody knew whose face had been seen. Was it the Prince of Wales's, the Queen's, the Prime Minister's? Whose face was it? No body knew.

Edgar J. Watkiss, with his roll of lead piping round his arm, said audibly, humorously of course: "The Proime Minister's kyar."

Septimus Warren Smith, who found himself unable to pass, heard him.

Septimus Warren Smith, aged about thirty, pale-faced, beak-nosed, wearing brown shoes and a shabby overcoat, with hazel eyes which had that look of apprehension in them which makes complete strangers apprehensive too. The world has raised its whip; where will it descend?

Everything had come to a standstill. The throb of the motor engines sounded like a pulse irregularly drumming through an entire body. The sun became extraordinarily hot because the motor car had stopped outside Mulberry's shop window; old ladies on the tops of omnibuses spread their black parasols; here a green, here a red parasol opened with a little pop. Mrs. Dalloway, coming to the window with her arms full of sweet peas, looked out with her little pink face pursed in enquiry. Everyone looked at the motor car. Septimus looked. Boys on bicycles sprang off. Traffic accumulated. And there the motor car stood, with drawn blinds, and upon them a curious pattern like a tree, Septimus thought, and this gradual drawing together of everything to one centre before his eyes, as if some horror had come almost to the surface and was about to burst into flames, terrified him. The world wavered and quivered and threatened to burst into flames. It is I who am blocking the way, he thought. Was he not being looked at and pointed at; was he not weighted there, rooted to the pavement, for a purpose? But for what purpose?

"Let us go on, Septimus," said his wife, a little woman, with large eyes in a sallow pointed face; an Italian girl.

You will have been struck by those intersections of different people, the ironies, the contrasts, the happy immunity of the lady buying her pink sweet peas apologized to by the shop woman because of the slight disturbance of the noise. The war-shocked man in his inner subjective torment—nobody's business except his wife's—at bay in his own strange unhappy world. The sublime, idealized, sentimental mystery surrounding the car, and, at the same time, the slight feeling of satire towards it: what *does* go on behind those grey blinds? And the mind moved also away from Bond Street, with that idea of cloud moving over roofs, moving even while the words go on towards the green hills of Hampstead, rising beyond London. It is an extraordinary drawing together in the moment, in the actuality of the Now, of the fortunes and the thoughts and the destinies of persons who gradually we are to follow as the day and the book goes on.

And while I am discussing time, in its sense of creating a sharp Now, I want to make clear the importance of the actual scene which time can create. The hour of the day, the season of the year, whether it rains or the sun shines; all these give what I have called actuality and sharpness to the moment of the scene as described. We depend a great deal on the time-information which the novelist gives to us. Think what a difference there is between a street and a street in the middle of the night; a seaside town and a seaside town in the autumn gales. One of the master scene-setters was Charles Dickens. To remind you of that I want you to consider an extract from *Bleak House*.

The waters are out in Lincolnshire. An arch of the bridge in the park has been sapped and sopped away. The adjacent low-lying ground, for half a mile in breadth, is a stagnant river, with melancholy trees for islands in it, and a surface punctured all over, all day long, with falling rain. My Lady Dedlock's "place" has been extremely dreary. The weather, for many a day and night, has been so wet that the trees seem wet through, and the soft loppings and prunings of the woodman's axe can make no crash or crackle as they fall. The deer, looking soaked, leave quagmires where they pass. The shot of a rifle loses its sharpness in the moist air, and its smoke moves in a tardy little cloud toward the green rise, coppice-topped, that makes a background for the falling rain. The view from my Lady Dedlock's own windows is alternately a lead-coloured view, and a view in Indian ink. The vases on the stone terrace in the foreground catch the rain all day; and the heavy drops fall, drip, drip, drip, upon the broad flagged pavement, called, from old time, the Ghost's Walk, all night. On Sundays, the little church in the park is mouldy; the oaken pulpit breaks out into a cold sweat, and there is a general smell and taste as of the ancient Dedlocks in their graves. My Lady Dedlock (who is childless), looking out in the early twilight from her boudoir at a keeper's lodge, and seeing the light of a fire upon the latticed panes, and smoke rising from the chimney, and a child, chased by a woman, running out into the rain to meet the shining figure of a wrapped-up man coming through the gate, has been put quite out of temper. My Lady Dedlock says she has been "bored to death."

There has been not only a physical scene, a landscape in heavy rain, but also a social scene. We have been given our first clue as to the secret of Lady Dedlock, and all that has been done in terms of the weather and the time of day. There is a close relation between the emotional effect of the atmosphere and the crisis of the character. Dickens has given us a scene by which any woman of fashion might well be what Lady Dedlock says she is—bored; but there is more to it. We are to know, as the story goes on, why she minds, why she is really tormented by, the sight of the child. And Dickens speaks of the rain-muffled axe blows and rifle shots, but his sentences are like blows or rifle shots which are not muffled. It is sharp, it is wonderfully actual, clean-cut; all that which stands out through the veil of rain.

Next, let us look at the question of time as timing: the expansion of some scenes—it may be a few moments—into pages; also, the contraction of long passages of time which must be felt to have passed and yet which are not actually described. The novelist, to a certain extent, opens and shuts time like a fan as he goes along—and this is important because every story demands (because of its proportion) some particular sort of timing of its own. There must be an allotment, a proportioning of time: timing gives emphasis, as you will understand. The few moments in which we may stop and stare at some face passing at the other side of the street, or the moments in which our eyes will dwell on some particular line of print in a newspaper. . . . All that demarcates that something important, though maybe only important to us, is occurring.

I would suggest that one reason why some novels, not bad—often making a good opening or a good start—lose their hold on us, is that as the plot goes on we feel the author losing his or her grip on actuality. There is a sort of slurring and we become impatient; we look back; we say: "Yes, but is this happening on a Tuesday or a Thursday?" We feel that the focus in which time should be has been lost, the thing is being mishandled. In a great novel, in a Tolstoi or a Balzac or a Trollope novel, I am certain that the author keeps in his mind that calendar on the wall, that clock on the table. Timing is the final important aspect of time *inside* the novel (on which I should like to leave time in that first class).

Now for time *outside* the novel. I am considering, as I suggested at the beginning, a time which is personal to us, which surrounds us like a climate or an atmosphere. It is time which is a page—or at any rate two or three lines—of history; although in the foreground, inevitably for most of us, stand the concerns and anxieties or the pleasures and fulfilments of each our own individual days. And all this rootedness of the reader in his own time does inevitably affect his attitude to the novel he reads and his sense of whether or not it contains a reality. I have a respect for people who say point-blank that they are attracted only by what is contemporary. They do not care for an "old" book. They feel alienated in some way by a time atmosphere or time climate which is not their own.

I thought of an instance of that in connection with the extract from *Mrs. Dalloway*. Why on earth, as we visualize a London street *now*, should there be any question of parasols or umbrellas opening on a top deck? The answer is that *Mrs. Dalloway* was written in 1925, and in 1925—as people of my generation will remember—the top deck of a bus was not roofed in. That, if it is not explained, can cause a shock to the sense of reality, to the reader of that passage. "No!" they would be inclined to call out. "That's wrong; that disturbs that picture in my mind, in my eye." And there are other, more fundamental changes. The judgments or the proportion may seem wrong. We may perceive what seem to us absurdities or perhaps bad practices, which were totally taken for granted in their own day. The heroines of Jane Austen, brilliant and charming as they are, may seem to us to be unduly concerned with getting themselves or their friends married. The great Thomas Hardy characters may seem overdrawn, made too gigantic, on the strength of what we now know about rural conditions in the south-west of England. The Henry James cosmopolitan, upper-class characters flit, it may seem, far too easily from capital to capital—they have no currency problems and apparently not many of them have any work to do. We must admit that a book originating in a time different from our own has certain differences of circumstance, and occasionally those differences may put up a sort of barrier between ourselves who read now and the novel and what is contained in it.

If that is so, or if that were so completely, how is it that any novels survive their time? I would say that a novel survives because of its basic truthfulness, its having within it something general and universal, and a quality of imaginative perception which applies just as much now as it did in the fifty or hundred or two hundred years since the novel came to life. A novel with force in it is durable, but the key is this thing to which I referred originally when we began these talks —the initial power to pierce through the surface to some cogent and important and general imaginative truth, about life, about experience, about human persons. A novel which survives, which withstands and outlives time, does do something more than merely survive. It does not stand still. It accumulates round itself the understanding of all these persons who bring to it something of their own. It acquires associations, it becomes a form of experience in itself, so that two people who meet can often make friends, find an approach to each other, because of this one great common experience they have had. And, like all experiences, it is added to by the power of different kinds of people in different times, to feel and to comment and to explain.

What about the novels of our day? I suggested in two or three places, such as in my remarks on the changes in the manner of the dialogue and the liking for dialogue, that evolution and change and alteration in the form of the novel is going on. It always has been, and, please heaven, it always will. I think the novel will be perfectly all right if it moves forward in time along with us.

We ask: What is the actuality in a novel written this year or last year, or a few years ago, which holds us? Is it perhaps a comprehension and a realization of our own time? Is it that—because of the stress of history and the extending consciousness we have of being people in a time—we are more time-conscious, we are more aware of the particular climate of our day? And therefore, though we cannot ever lose our interest in individuals, is there this slight shifting of interest from the individual to the circumstance, to the individual and the relation between him and others, which compose and make for society? And when I speak of a novel being truly contemporary I do not mean the purely topical, which bases itself on the events or happenings of one year. We want our time to live in art and in the comprehension of other people, as the times before us lived for us; and I do not doubt for a moment that we are raising up and finding groups of artists, among them the novelist no less than the poet, who will express the feeling and values of our day and at the same time seize what there is in it that is fundamental, the thing which has come from the past and will pass on into the future—in fact, universal human experience.

Novelists now have to take in, to express, to comprehend, an enormous mass of new things. It is no good pretending that the circumstances of human life and the background of human judgment are not very different from what they were fifty years ago, and for this expression a particular kind of vocabulary may have to be found, a vocabulary not only of language but of ideas. There must be language, and a language that can be kept open at the edges, and if our young novelists are to exist, if they are to survive, they do need, I think, more attention and more response and more come-back on the part of the reader, than novelists have ever needed before. The relation between the writer and the reader is and needs to be closer than it has been. The writer needs reception, good reception in the radio sense, because of this forging ahead, this seeking for an expression which shall be unique to our age and yet hold in it the elements of all time. I ask you to look out for, to be aware of, the writers, the novelists, who seem to you to be making the literature of our age. Receive them, understand them, help them, and leave in our time, as there has been before, this close link, this identification, between fiction which we read and enjoy and the truths which through fiction we comprehend.

A NOTE ABOUT THE AUTHOR

BORN in Ireland, Elizabeth Bowen was early in life taken to England, where she received her schooling. In her twenties she discovered the rewards of travel, and her first novel, *The Hotel*, grew out of one of her early sojourns in Italy. In spite of the pleasure she has always derived from living abroad—including America, where she feels very much at home—her first allegiance is to County Cork, where her family settled after coming over from Wales in the seventeenth century.

Since the publication of her first short stories in 1923, Elizabeth Bowen has published four books of non-fiction, six collections of short stories, and eight novels, among them *To the North, The House in Paris, The Death of the Heart, The Heat of the Day,* and *A World of Love,* which have earned her a unique reputation.

In the Birthday Honours List of 1948, Elizabeth Bowen was created a Companion of the British Empire.

April 1962

A NOTE ON THE TYPE

THE TEXT of this book was set on the Linotype in a face called TIMES ROMAN, designed by Stanley Morison for *The Times* (LONDON), and first introduced by that newspaper in 1932. Among typographers and designers of the twentieth century, Stanley Morison has been a strong forming influence, as typographical adviser to the English Monotype Corporation, as a director of two distinguished English publishing houses, and as a writer of sensibility, erudition, and keen practical sense.

Composed, printed, and bound by
Kingsport Press, Inc., Kingsport, Tennessee.
Typography and binding design
based on originals by

WARREN CHAPPELL